THE BIRTH OF THE SHINING ONE: MOVING BEYOND APOCALYPSE INTO GODBEING

Joe Landwehr
Light of the Forest Primeval 1987

D0836150

Uni✳Sun
Kansas City

Request for such permission should be addressed to:

Uni★Sun
P.O. Box 25421
Kansas City, MO 64119

This book is manufactured in the United States of America. Distribution by The Talman Company.

The Tallman Company
150 Fifth Avenue
New York, NY 10011

ISBN # 0-912949-23-6
Library of Congress Catalog Card Number 88-051046

A
Uni★Sun
BOOK
Distributed by
THE TALMAN COMPANY

This book is dedicated to Connie Sutherland-Hernandez, whose unwavering support in the early days helped open a channel through which these words began to flow. From the Shining One within me to the Shining One within her goes my undying love and appreciation.

I would also like to express my appreciation to Josef Tornick for his sensitive editing skills, and his uncanny ability to mirror the truth of my own message back to me. Many thanks, as well, to Debra Oliver for her poignant honesty and capacity for asking just the right questions, to Bara Fischer for her heartfelt enthusiasm, and to all those friends who read my manuscript and added words of encouragement to my creative momentum.

CONTENTS

Foreword by Ken Carey

First impressions often stick with you. I will never forget the day I met Joe Landwehr. We'd had an especially hot Ozark summer that should have been turning to fall, but there was no let up in the intense heat. I was in the midst of a building project, constructing a solar-heated composting outhouse on our farm. I was hammering away with my brother Tom and son Bill, when Joe walked up to where we were working and introduced himself.

Many of our visitors in those days expected us to drop our work the moment they arrived, but Joe quietly picked up an extra hammer, put on a nail apron and lent an experienced hand as we talked and got to know one another. He had come all the way from Florida in response to an article he had read about an environmental project we were working on to prevent the clearcutting of 600 acres of hardwood forest between our home and the nearby river. Joe had come to help. And he lost no time in doing so. Here was a man after my own heart.

Joe not only helped us finish our construction project, he pitched right in on the environmental initiative as well. He was one of nine people who volunteered two years of their lives to protecting the oaks, hickory, walnut and dogwood trees that bless these forest-covered mountains. When our efforts succeeded and the Greenwood Forest Association was established, Joe was elected to serve a term as president.

For nearly three years, my family and I lived in community with Joe Landwehr, sharing meals, work, childcare, finances, music, sorrow, laughter and all the little things that go together to make up a life. Joe's particular gift—initially to those of us who lived and worked with him, and now thankfully to many thousands—is his ability to find words to express the vastness of the vibrational energies manifesting in the great

Universal Mother who surrounds and permeates our every moment.

Joe's Full Moon Meditations are masterpieces of perception and articulation, beautiful and eloquent renderings in clear and lucid language of that universal and eternal reality. Using his background in astrology, each month during this past decade he has mapped the course of the vibrational energies whose influence touches our walks upon this earth. Many times Sherry and I have read the latest Full Moon Meditation and have seen reflected there, in beautiful and poetic style, an exact mirror of the vibrational reality we were that month experiencing. At times like these we turn to each other and say, "How do you suppose he does that?"

Well, I do not know exactly how Joe does it, but I am glad that he does. It is a great pleasure to introduce this book and to see it sent out into the world where it can be appreciated by many. Those who read through the pages of this volume will find a confirmation of what they have intuitively felt to be true, and an empowerment to live that truth.

I have not lost sight of my first impression of Joe. Over the decade of our acquaintance it has proven its accuracy. He is a man who is willing to put himself on the line.

Sun Bear once said that if a philosophy does not grow corn, he is not interested in it. I agree. I am not interested in words and ideas that are not applied and lived. Joe lives what he believes. There is reality and substance to his words. He has something unique to offer to us all. He is a special friend, a brother, a co-worker. May *The Birth of the Shining One* succeed in touching many hearts. It is a powerful and insightful volume, designed to awaken in us what we have always known, but what we so often forget in this sensory land of wonder and challenge. I am happy to welcome its light into the world.

—Ken Carey
August 1988

INTRODUCTION:
DANCING THE DANCE OF
POST-APOCALYPTIC
JUBILATION

For some time now, many of us have been searching for a deeper connection to our spirituality. In a world of turbulent surface change, the possibility of communion with a more deeply grounded, peaceful part of ourselves became an attractive goal. In a world imbalanced by economic injustice, we sought the source of all abundance. In a world contaminated by socio-cultural biases and commercial distortions, we sought the uncontaminated truth. On a planet crucified by ecological insensitivity and mocked by the arrogance of corporate-industrial gargoyles, we began to worship the simple beauty of a sunrise and the balance of a flower. Somewhere along the line, our lives had become too complex, too cumbersome, and too carcinogenic, and we began turning toward more conscious alternatives.

In the late sixties, we had a great deal of longstanding frustration to vent, and so our quest took a more radical turn. We began by blasting the gates of our consciousness with psychedelic dynamite, and blowing the lid off our boxed-up version of reality. Light began to filter through the cracks in the wall, and we began to see dimly past the shadows what was really going on around us. The dam of our complacency finally broke, and outrage flooded through the streets of our cities like a school of hungry piranha stalking their prey. We hurled our fury at the ears of our faltering demagogues, and were able to bring our involvement in an insane war to an end. In doing so, we discovered our collective power, but also opened forever a Pandora's box of long neglected social injustices: minority oppression, patriarchal tyranny, ecological rape, political deceit, commercial exploitation, nutritional toxification, medical tyranny, brainwashing at the hands of our educational systems, and manipulation by our media.

Overwhelmed by it all, we collapsed in upon ourselves - exhausted, but comforted by the dawning realization that the world began at our doorstep. In order to effect significant change out there, it was obvious we would have to begin by sweeping our own house clean.

Throughout the seventies, we employed a wide variety of brooms. We travelled to the temples of distant lands, and brought back exotic fragrances and magic syllables. We twisted our bodies into foreign postures, and deprived ourselves of food. We imbibed the twinkling words of soft-spoken holy men, and donned the garb of full-time seekers, unperturbed in our affected serenity. Then tiring of our imported gurus, we returned to our own bedraggled heritage, the prodigal sons and daughters of Western culture, looking once again to mine the diamonds in our own backyard. We began to weep and pound our way across the pillowed floors of psychologized America, and drag out our skeletons for display. We encountered and mirrored ourselves in secret places, rubbed each other raw with concern and confrontation, and salved our open wounds with newfound self-acceptance. We learned to run for the sheer joy of running, and began to celebrate the circulation of revitalized blood through our veins.

Stepping back into our lives, we could now see more clearly what needed to be done. Armed with fresh commitment, we grew in political savvy and learned to go about the momentous task of giving our vision form without getting side-swiped by the careening dinosaur of industrialized civilization. We were ready to suffer the rigors of our own personal withdrawal from centuries of fossil fuel addiction, and take responsibility for our rightful stewardship of natural systems. We were ready to give each other the space we needed to be free and equal in the dance of our differences, and look for local solutions to local problems. We were beginning to reclaim our power, and teach each other what we had learned in our years of reaching inward. We took it upon ourselves to build more efficient shelters, grow more vibrant food, nurture more loving relationships, simplify our needs, pool our resources, evolve more responsive communities, and raise more conscious children.

The old order was still rumbling along in its clamor and confusion, snorting out soot and negativity. But in the glistening
dawn of the new world we were birthing, we were content to
dwell in the coziness of our alternate reality, gazing out in
reverie at a parallel dimension gone mad.

In the eighties, some of us have retreated to a numbing
cocoon of material distraction, attempting to escape the horror
of an increasingly desecrated environment, volatile relationships between nations, corporate irresponsibility, and epi-
demic diseases. Others have intensified the quest, turning to
discarnate beings, ancient tribal rites, and global displays of
mass consciousness for workable answers.

While entire nations of people starve *en masse*, millions of
people around the world rally to buy food. While primeval
rainforests are destroyed so Americans can eat cheap ham-
burger, others chain themselves to trees, and place their lives
between sea mammals and the harpoon. While the weaponry
of yesterday's science fiction finds its way out among the stars,
the planetary nervous system gets ignited by the wizardry of
the microchip. As our world threatens to self-destruct, increasing numbers of us awaken to a more consciously activated
state of empowerment, as well as a more global sense of responsibility. Radical times have precipitated catalytic action
on a scale never before imagined.

Yet, as far as we have come in our journey toward claiming
our power and our freedom, as we step off toward the nineties,
we must not underestimate the challenge of the road ahead.
The work of transformation demands far more than an occasional empowered act, or the mere recognition of Spirit
operating beneath the surface of our lives.

The time has come for us to realize that we *are* Spirit moving
with full power through human form. We *are* the gods and
goddesses to whom we pray. We *are* the *bodhisattvas*, returning
to grace the planet with our compassion. We *are* the Christ
returned to Earth.

The salvation we long for is our birthright. But this salvation can be guaranteed only insofar as we are willing to
create it for ourselves. Only as we claim our godbeing, can
we put the threat of apocalypse behind us, and move into a
world that is worthy of our holy presence. This is the challenge
before us now. The apocalypse, cryptically portrayed in the

Bible, and often interpreted as a prophecy of destruction, is simply the passing away of all that is grounded in limitation and fear. To the extent that we have purged our lives of fear, we have already moved through the transition apocalypse is meant to bring.

It is our job now to move through whatever fear remains, and to demonstrate in our living what it is like to be alive and well after the apocalypse has come and gone. There may still be this parallel dimension truly going mad, but where is the nook or cranny in this post-apocalyptic world of ours that does not contain a glimmer of the light, a whisper of the truth, a reflection of the plan revealed? As we begin to feel this reality within our bones, and live its implications in our lives, we become our own salvation. There is no other way.

Whatever the planetary melodrama may bring, in the end it is Spirit that will triumph. To the extent that we have claimed our godbeing, and left our fear behind, we will dance at the victory celebration. Regardless of the costumes we choose to wear, or who we think our partners are, or where we think the dance is going, it is all one dance we do. Let us grab the apocalyptic beast by its paws and set it dancing to the rhythm of its own heartbeat, to the sweet serenade of its own divinity. Let us keep turning round until the world turns with us. Let us teach the dance of post-apocalyptic jubilation to everyone we touch, until even in the heart of that parallel dimension gone mad, it's the only dance in town.

1

TOWARD THE BIRTH
OF THE SHINING ONE

Within the reader of this book dwells a Being of Light. It is to this Being of Light that these words are addressed, for this Being of Light is who You really are, regardless of the outer forms you have chosen momentarily to inhabit. Because you have become so identified with these forms You are moving through, you have forgotten Who it is that moves and why You have chosen to do so. You have mistaken the movement, in all of its myriad manifestations, for the Life Energy that has the power to create such manifestations in the first place. Yet, You are not these forms. You are Life Energy Itself. Although You momentarily choose to move through particular forms, You are in no way limited or defined by appearances. You are a Being of Light. You are Spirit. You are the One who has created this planetary passion play, seeking to take birth more consciously within these forms you inhabit.

You have chosen to incarnate on this planet so that Earth Itself might play Its part within a divine plan that extends far beyond the power of the human mind to comprehend. As a Being of Light, You remember this plan. You eat, drink, and breathe its essence as You go about your work here upon the Earth. As a human being you have forgotten who You are and the part you were meant to play. You have become entranced instead by the world of form that appears to surround you.

In our collective forgetfulness, we have all but destroyed the vehicle through which our mission was to be accomplished. We have ravaged our forests, squandered our topsoil, polluted our rivers and oceans, and in places, rendered our atmosphere unfit to breathe. We can do better than this. We can remember our sacred mandate, and get on with the task at hand. Surely these words resonate somewhere deep within you, and open a pathway through which You can emerge in the full radiance of Your Being, and Your Glory.

You are poised, alone, but also together with us all, on the threshold of new birth. You have been here, in this place of anticipation, many times before. It is a place where the intensity of momentous change easily overwhelms the conscious mind and floods the heart with a strange, but powerful effusion of deeply rooted grief and trembling joy.

It is a place in which the inevitability of death calls an end to the various games you have been playing at your leisure, and life shines with a newness that obliterates all memory of the history of your passage. There is a snap in consciousness, in this place of death, that disrupts your accustomed way of being in the world just long enough for you to realize unmistakably the true nature of this human experiment that has engaged Your boundless creativity.

This realization has always been available at the time of physical death, for it is here that the veils between form and essence are thinnest. In this time of accelerated planetary transformation, the veils between form and essence are thinning for us all. *You need no longer wait for physical death to have the realization of Your True Identity,* for every major change or life experience that fully engages your attention affords you this same opportunity. The loss of a job, or a loved one, a powerful dream, a peak of loving sexual pleasure, a quiet moment of reflection on the beauty of a sunset - any of these, indeed any moment in which you are fully present and aware, can be a doorway through which the boundaries between forms dissolve, and You enter more completely into Your own Holy Presence.

In these moments, you have an important choice to make.

You can either identify with the experience through which Spirit has travelled, or you can identify with Spirit. If you choose to identify with experience, the snap in consciousness that accompanies the fully present moment will bring only a sense of loss, disorientation, and disempowerment, after the experience has passed. You will not understand the Shining that accompanies your emergence on the other side of the snap. In time, the Shining will fade, and you will find yourself once again at the beginning, a restless, but ill-defined longing unconsciously propelling your trial-and-error movement toward the next threshold opportunity.

If, on the other hand, you choose to identify with Spirit, You will emerge on the other side of the snap in consciousness as the Shining Itself, a Reality that can and will not fade, though the forms that house It come and go with the endless passing of seasons. As the Shining One, You bring continuous threshold opportunity into the lives of those you touch with your own. You generate a Presence in which the longing for enlightenment far outweighs any need for the protection and preservation of form.

It is time to prepare a welcome for the Shining One, for the moment of Birth is at hand. You must be impeccably clear about what it is you are choosing in each moment. You must be vigilant so that Essence might emerge unclouded through each experience, each cycle of circumstance, each relationship, each threshold opportunity you encounter. You must be willing to let go of each form as it has served its purpose. You must learn to see the Light at the heart of each form you encounter without mistaking the form for the Reality that it houses. You must gather and release Light effortlessly, shining in all directions at once, clinging nowhere. Ultimately, you must know Yourself within all form, indeed as the Source of form itself; for as the Shining One, this is who You are.

We have all been under the spell of the world of form for far too long, caught by the illusion of separation, waxing dangerous in our folly. The breaking of this spell will precipitate reconvergence among sisters and brothers of like Spirit, wise ones all, each bearing special gifts to the Shining One being born, and from the Shining One to us. The breaking of this spell will precipitate the healing of the Earth.

2

ON THE JOURNEY ACROSS
THE CHASM OF LIGHT

Each of us has within us a driving passion to go beyond our own sense of limitation. This passion varies from individual to individual according to our nature. Depending upon our level of self-acceptance and the capacity of those around us to accommodate us in the fullness of our being, this passion may or may not ultimately come to characterize our lives. By whatever name this passion is called, however, and to whatever extent it is allowed to flow through us, it is the same omnipresent Spirit that animates us all and underlies our every expression in the world of form.

As we become willing to live our lives with passion, to dare to go beyond the limitations we have imposed upon ourselves thus far, we become infused with this animating Spirit. We come into our power as individuals, and at the same time, experience an increasing sense of connection with other individuals. The barriers between us begin to dissolve, and Light begins to fill the cracks in the walls that separate one form from another. Gradually, as we allow our passion to move us forward, we let go our identification with form and begin to identify with this Light.

Yet, in the transition from form to Light, we are faced with an awesome dilemma. We straddle two sides of an ever-widening chasm. On one side are the old forms, the old identity through which we have begun to experience our Essence. On the other is *always* another possibility within the world of form, a more evolved reality, a definite step forward, but a step that is not without risk. In the chasm itself lies the Light we are glimpsing in ever increasing intensity; the Light that threatens to consume us should we surrender to it completely, but which draws us in spite of ourselves; the Light we have been seeking so earnestly, but which in truth, we cannot bear to look directly in the face.

Our dilemma is plain and painful. We can't go back, for the side of the chasm from which we come is crumbling beneath our feet. Yet to leap to the other side is to abandon our security, to relinquish our identity, to face the holy terror of the unknown. We are lured by the possibility of greater freedom, but there is much we stand to lose. We like to think we can trust our intuitions, and are forever moving toward our highest good, but in the end, there can be no guarantees. Yet, the longer we wait, the more perilous our identification with these old familiar forms. The longer we wait, the more inevitable our landslide with these forms into the chasm of Light.

It is as though we are on a boat sailing rapidly away from a harbor enveloped in fog. Once we reach the open sea, we can no longer be entirely sure that the harbor is still there. We wonder whether or not it might be wise to return, given the unclear conditions surrounding our journey. Yet, in seriously considering such a move, we inevitably decide to keep going, though perhaps at a slower pace, because an immediate return to a foggy harbor would be more dangerous than moving on.

So it is with our lives. The forms that have given meaning to our journey thus far, and connect us to the past, no longer provide a reliable link to this present moment. In fact, they often seduce us into dangerous alliance with that which is passing away. To look back at this point, and especially to seriously consider going back, is to court disaster. As uncertain and dangerous as the journey before us seems at times to be, it is our only viable option.

This foggy limbo in which we find ourselves, where neither past nor future exists in dependable clarity, is really the compassionate gift of Spirit. It is given to us so that we may sharpen our attention in the present moment. In the present moment and only in the present moment is the door to our safe haven, the still voice of clear guidance, the unfailing hand of the well-seasoned Cosmic Traveller to help us on our way. Within each one of us is an infallible compass, set with exquisite precision toward our destination. Before we entered these physical realms, We set this compass ourselves, so We would not get lost within the illusion of form. Now, whenever we quiet ourselves enough to fully enter the present moment, this compass reliably points in the direction of our next step.

Because the fog of mass consciousness around us now is thick, and the atmosphere wildly sensitive and volatile, this compass leads us so very tenderly, small step by small step, lest we trigger by unduly precipitate action, an irreversible chain of cumulative disaster. We need only slow ourselves down and attune ourselves to the scale on which meaningful change is still inching us toward our destination in order to find our way through the fog.

On this scale of movement, which can only be measured from within as the crumbling of perceptual walls separating one form from another, energy is released for the healing and regeneration of the outer world. As we relinquish our separation, and remember our interconnection with all of life, we begin to see the light between the cracks of that which is crumbling all around us. We facilitate the release of light throughout the world of form. We allow this light to permeate our lives.

This release of light is the baptism by fire written about in scriptures, not the violent disintegration of form that grabs our attention from the headlines. As we affirm this release of light in the passing of our connection to the past, we release ourselves from the external melodrama to live again in light. It is here that all children of Spirit move forward in harmony and triumph, even through the dream fog, across an uncertain open sea of time/timelessness, toward a destination we realize to be beneath our feet in our awakening.

The intensity we experience in the crossing is only due to the fact that the rules by which we navigate are not the rules we remember from our training on the shore. Though many could sense the coming of the transitional journey, and some found solace in imagining a destination, none could predict beforehand what the actual conditions on the open sea would require us to know. At best, our external teachers and guides were able to point us in the right direction. As we followed their relatively illuminated fingers, life itself would release small details for our assimilation. But the journey itself is somewhat different than we have imagined, more changeable from moment to moment, more demanding of our resourcefulness, spontaneity, and adaptability.

Survival no longer depends upon what we have managed to learn, or think we know, but upon our ability to stay focused in the eye of the storm, to identify with the core of Light in each molecule of fog, to hear the pure tone of celestial welcome clearly amid the cacophony of drowning panic all around us. This is not to say that what we know will not prove useful, but rather that only as we remain clear of preconceived notions in the moment will the appropriate tools present themselves for our use. As we lock our concentration into the light that draws us, our inner compass will effect optimum navigation, steering us into experience designed to disintegrate whatever inner walls remain.

This journey we have been impelled to embark upon from the beginning of conscious time will stretch each and every one of us to the point of maximum resiliency. The very concept of form, as that within which we might package our lives, may soon no longer be relevant, except on the most superficial level of experience. Heretofore seemingly inviolable boundaries will dissolve with increasing rapidity, and Spirit will be free to follow newly opened channels of passage with greater spontaneity. This is a natural expansion culminating in the liberating recognition of the omnipresence of Spirit within each one of us and the interconnectedness of all seemingly separate form.

Wherever we do not feel large enough to contain this expansion, we cling to the familiar boundaries of the form world with attachment. More often than not the changes we are impelled to make call us to a higher level of functioning, but the attachments we form in insecurity and fear hold us back. The discomfort we often feel on the edge of change is usually due to this attachment, rather than to the change itself. In spite of these attachments, the heat that is generated through our resistance to change burns through our clinging and moves us inexorably toward a surrender of our attachments for the sake of growth. In this way, as we move through life, we continuously shed the forms that we have outgrown, and move into larger forms capable of housing the expanded Spirit moving through us.

Taking this process to its extreme, the earth itself is a form which we must one day relinquish to the passage of Spirit beyond all bounds of limitation.

Even as light flows into light without the least visible trace of boundary, so will the Shining One emerge through each form and claim this world as Its own.

What we are faced with under such conditions, is our own psychological death. It is a death that brings with it the possibility of utter transformation, but also no guarantee. How attached are we to the forms that have brought us to the very edge of transformation? How much of our identity is tied to that which is passing? If we can remain faithful to the Spirit moving through these forms, even as the forms themselves change with increasing rapidity, we will also change in ways that are incomprehensible to us now.

Yet, even as our identification with Spirit grows, we continue to be faced with choices within the realm of form.

We make these choices as consciously as we can. Yet, who can say, as the precipice draws near, that the choices we make in forming our worldly allegiances are right? Only time will tell, and in the end it may be that time does nothing but echo laughter in our crumbling faces. It is a time to hold firm to our intentions and be courageous in their execution, but it is also a time to be ready, if need be, to shrug with the gods, and start again from scratch.

At the very least, it is time to subject our attachments to the acid test of spiritual relevance. It may be we have been deluding ourselves. If so, our delusion will be made clear through the pain we experience indulging our involvement with forms that are trying to pass away. On the other hand, as our level of attachment changes, we may find ourselves moving through a world suddenly opened up to deeper meaning. We may happily discover a formlessness within form, a timelessness within time, an eternal light within the dancing shadows.

As this change takes place, history will rewrite itself in the eyes of those who have chosen to identify with Spirit. All will be re-interpreted within a context of planetary evolution, and all seemingly destructive or negative events will be understood as part of a global cleansing process. For those who have been choosing identification with form, this cleansing will be most intense. For those who have consistently refused to pay attention, an agonizing process of disintegration will begin, although through the eyes of Spirit, even this can be seen as a creative release of poorly bound energy for more appropriate application. For those who have chosen to identify with Spirit, however, there will be ecstatic communion with the essence of all form, and joyous celebration of a new world washed clean once again.

This is a hard time for those who have long tried to identify with Spirit, for there are no maps pointing to the place were

Spirit eternally dwells. These are times in which nothing is sacred, but sacredness itself. Where the heart is open, the mystery can reveal itself; but where the heart is closed, no amount of devotion to ceremony, ritual, or sanctified form can invoke it. Wherever the form has been mistaken for the possibility inherent in the form, the fool will emerge with the egg of spiritual ego on his face. But wherever the Spirit has been truly followed through Its ever-changing relationship with particular forms, those form will soon be shed as a butterfly sheds its cocoon, and the exquisite, ineffable beauty of life's unfathomable mystery will be revealed.

3

THE QUEST FOR STABLE
IDENTITY

Most of us look to the world of form for our security. Very few even bother to question that the flow of circumstances and events that mark our days is what our lives are all about. Yet many of us have also noticed that none of these forms or circumstances provide much real security at all. There is nothing manifest in the realm of circumstance that is not subject to rapid, unpredictable, and radical change, especially in these days of accelerated planetary transformation. The revolution in self-understanding precipitated by the human potentials movement, the snowballing climax of technological prowess, the hyperactive economic climate, and the ascending stakes of international power politics all contribute toward a highly volatile atmosphere of runaway change. There is very little that can be taken for granted, and nothing that we can look to as an absolute reference point. The rules are constantly changing, and each one of us must discover what those changes are for ourselves. There are no outside authorities who know. Even those we have looked to as our prophets and teachers can only take us to the edge of our own transformation, where general trends based on probabilities often do not easily apply.

The real difficulty, however, does not lie with the constantly changing melodrama of external circumstance. It lies with our attempts to maintain a stable sense of identity through identification with that which is passing away.

In the old days, before the transition to this new age of conscious alignment began, identity was quite naturally a function of life circumstance. Many of us had a relatively stable job, married someone we expected to stay with for a lifetime, often lived in the same town from cradle to grave, belonged to a particular church, and in general, realized our identity through the choices we made about the circumstances of our lives. Be-

11

yond the freak accident, unforeseen twist of fate, or act of divine intervention, there was a tangible sense of continuity to life that one could count on. A relatively stable identity was obtainable through identification with circumstances. Indeed, such an identity was the end product of the normal course of progression through life.

But now, as the evolutionary process intensifies and accelerates, it no longer makes sense to identify with forms that we outgrow almost before we try them on. The job we held last year may well have been rendered obsolete this year through some technological breakthrough. The happy marriage we had hoped to settle into might find two loving individuals whose growth needs take them in opposite directions. The old hometown has long since revealed its mysteries and lost its novelty and charm. And the church simply does not address itself to the needs of Spirit burning from within to express its living truth through our lives. The world beyond our doorstep is wracked with terrorism, nuclear disaster, widespread contamination by toxic chemicals, precarious relationships between nations, economic malaise, and cultural vacuity. Nothing stable there.

As a species, we have already taken the stable identity of circumstance as far as it can go. Spirit is moving faster now and the pace does not often allow time for circumstances to gel. We are changing inside faster than outer circumstances can reveal. Pretending that the circumstances in which we momentarily dwell define who we are can only perpetuate the illusion of outer continuity at the expense of inner integrity.

Eventually there comes a split between who we are inside, and what our lives reveal about us. The strain that it takes to maintain circumstances that no longer fit catapults us outward into the very change we have tried to avoid, and we move on in spite of ourselves. Holding back to preserve some external semblance of order or continuity only creates a larger mess in the end, as Spirit finally shatters the bulging forms, and dramatically destroys what was only meant to fade away of its own accord.

Outer reality no longer contains the substance of stable identity, because outer reality is in a state of accelerated flux. We are in a planetary centrifuge, whirling at breakneck speed toward the cutting edge of our familiar reality. There is no place solid outside ourselves to cling, and everything that once held tight now flies to the wind.

Behind this rapid flux of circumstance, however, is a purpose. We are learning, some by choice, and many by necessity, to look to a deeper place than circumstance for our identity. We no longer identify with the job that we hold, but with the creativity within that demands expression. We no longer define ourselves through our relationships, but through the love and the joy within that demand to be shared. The town we live in, the church we belong to, and the political party to which we pledge our affiliation no longer determine who we are. Instead it is our inner sense of purpose, and our longing for community that form and reform, abandon and create anew the world of social institutions through which we move.

Realizing that the stable identity we seek cannot be found in circumstances, we are free to let them go as they serve our purpose. No longer attached to the external reality that has defined (and limited) us, we are free to create and re-create our circumstances according to the inner promptings of the moment. It may be our prompting is still to pursue the stable job, the lasting marriage, and all the other outer trappings of circumstantial security. Nonetheless, our movement toward these goals will be determined by the growth needs of Spirit moving through us, not by what we think we want. On the other hand, it may just as likely be that our promptings move us to quit the stable job in order to pursue the call of some less certain adventure more directly connected to our passion, or to forgo the lasting marriage to deal more openly with issues of vulnerability and trust.

Many of us may find ourselves cast through life as through a series of increasingly vivid dreams. With each successive dream, we awaken with greater freedom to move on to the next, the old dissolving forms releasing once again our creativity for higher application. At each stage of the process, circumstances will change to reflect our level of awakening.

The identity we honor as we allow these changes will be no less real or solid to us than that we would attain by clinging to circumstances for our security, and perhaps a good deal more abiding. Leaving our attachment to circumstances behind, we identify with the Source of all circumstances, and are free to enter the entrancement of the world of form at will. In this freedom, we shall find the security that we seek, the only security there can ever really be.

4

FROM CRUCIFIED TO CROSSMAKER

The realm of circumstance is inevitably characterized by problems. We are forever seeking to rearrange our lives to better meet our needs, and when our needs cannot easily be met, a problem is encountered. We perceive some lack, limitation, or undesirable situation outside ourselves to be the source of our difficulty, and proceed as though something external to the self must be changed.

In reality, the circumstance is never the problem.

What we call the problem is always a mirror reflection of a more fundamental imbalance in our attitude. When we get locked into seeing our lives problematically, we fail to recognize the gateway through which Spirit fills our lives more completely. We fail to appreciate the gifts we are being given, fail to see the perfection, the abundance, and the blessings that always surround us.

The circumstances of our lives simply are what they are. It is our attitude toward them, and not the externals that determine our experience. Any situation in which we find ourselves can either be an opening through which Spirit enters our lives with greater Presence, or an obstacle in our path, depending on how we look at it. We are not victims. There is a conscious choice to be made.

Wherever we feel limited by circumstances, it is time to take another look. It may be all that is required to "solve" our problem is a willingness to see everything that happens as a necessary step along the road to our inevitable liberation. Any other way of looking at life keeps us forever separate from that which we deeply aspire to be. When we choose to see life problematically, problem after problem will arise to stand in our way. It is inevitable, for that is what we are creating. When we choose to see each difficulty as a gateway through which we can move more consciously into identification with Spirit, then we free ourselves from our bondage to the world of form. This is equally inevitable, provided we are willing to give up having problems. In truth, there are no problems. We already are that which we deeply aspire to be. Every circumstance, every event, every difficulty we encounter is our invitation to be the godbeing that we are. Nothing can stand between us and our godbeing except our own denial. We can choose to frame our experience problematically, if we do not feel ready to claim our power, but power unclaimed will ultimately work against us. Insisting upon our bondage, it is only a matter of time before the lock to our prison door rusts shut.

Certainly there has been great emphasis throughout the history of human culture upon the solution of problems. It can reasonably be argued that most breakthrough discoveries in science; most social, political, religious and economic reforms; and many cultural developments have evolved as a quest for solution to to some problem. Many of the great people remembered by historians are those who have seemingly devoted their lives to problem-solving. Yet, with all of the creative genius expended in this direction, we might wonder why it is that there are as least as many, undoubtedly more problems now that there were before our ancestors ever discovered the use of fire and started us on this journey. Not only are there more problems, but the problems we have now are more complex and more intertwined with other problems than they ever have been. Where has this emphasis on problems led but to bigger and better problems? From time to time there have been those who suggested that there might be another way to approach this dilemma.

Artists, musicians and craftspeople, at least those not strictly focused on commercial success, have traditionally allowed the emergence of Spirit through their art to take precedence over practical considerations. In their passing, may of them have left a legacy of upliftment and beauty to counterbalance our cultural preoccupation with problems.

Those like Emerson, Thoreau, or Muir, who have spent much time in natural settings, simply observing and experiencing, without needing to change or improve the handiwork of nature, have also left a legacy of appreciation that moves the soul to wonder and contentment. Saints and sages throughout the ages have suggested that where Spirit was given precedence above all else, the natural order and rhythm of life would ensure that practical needs were automatically taken care of. Christ in particular, told us that if we sought first the kingdom of heaven, all else would be granted unto us.

The sad fact is that few of these voices crying out through a wilderness of problem solvers have really been heard. Artists, musicians and craftspeople with integrity must often struggle against the prevailing tides of a cultural climate oriented toward commercial success. Those who deeply appreciate the natural environment for its own sake have been compelled to wage war against the technological problem-solvers in response to some crisis in order to be heard. Saints and sages have often heard their message drown in the clamor of the personality cult that followed them, and spiritual insight has become a commodity to be bought and sold on the open market.

Christ, it is said, died for our sins, and solved the problem of denied entry into heaven for the masses. Yet, from another perspective, Christ died because he dared to suggest that attunement to Spirit might ultimately be more profitable than the quest for higher circumstance. Is it not part of our unspoken cultural psychology that those who shift their focus from worldly matters to the inner life must either withdraw from society or be ostracized? Among those of us who consciously make spiritual attunement a priority in the midst of busy worldly lives, how many of us assume a dichotomy between the two? How many of us secretly fear the crucifixion we have been taught must come when our True Selves are revealed through all we say and do? Yet, in taking physical birth, each of us has already been crucified on our own personal cross of circumstance.

On the level of pure Spirit, before birth, we saw what it would take to inspire us to relinquish our attachment to form, and arranged our own crucifixion. And now, in this crucified state, we have a choice. We can either hang, immobilized by the problem our cross imposes, or move through the gateway at the heart of our predicament into the Presence of our own divinity. Christ did rise again from the dead, demonstrating in that most unsubtle act how each of us might also transcend the crucified, problematic state.

On the level of the problem, the cross on which we hang inevitably becomes the instrument of our torture. We feel the searing pain of the nails where they have torn our flesh, and recoil in the face of our own mortality. We endure the relentless desert sun against our throbbing brain, and pray for a swift lapse into the darkness of death. We sense the circling of buzzards overhead, and only hope that we can escape our body before they begin their tactless and bloody feast. There is no room in such a scenario for us to rise above our circumstances, because we are thoroughly identified with the crucified form that is now passing. All seems senseless and trite, a mockery of the accumulated identity we have invested in what came before.

If on the other hand, we could feel our crucifixion as the passing of one form into another, we would find a gateway into other worlds, even in the midst of our pain.

Instead of the ebbing of our body's strength, we would feel the empowerment of nail piercing flesh. We would become the sun itself, radiating light, generating heat, drawing forth the green of leaf and the reddish brown of baking earth, mediating life and death in our intensity. We would fly with the buzzards, feel the wind against our wings, and feed upon the very bones we once called our own, but now surrender. Letting go of this crucified body, nothing would be lost, for the same Life Force that moved us before would move us again in new ways, in wondrous variety, and endless exploration of form after form after form.

Through this exploration, shedding one body after another, we would gradually come to know ourselves as that which underlies all form, that which endures regardless of our movement from one form to the next. We would realize that underlying all apparent change is simply the emergence or unclouding of Essence. Crucified body, cross, sun, and buzzard would all be one continuum, all part of the same revelation of Essence. We could no longer give credence to the problematic state, because we would know ourselves as Crossmaker, as well as crucified.

As Crossmaker, we can afford to laugh at our problems.

If we identify not only with this crucified body in which we dwell, but also with the Source of whatever "problem" we perceive - whether it be crucifixion, a flat tire, an angry spouse, or nuclear waste - we know the problem to be a gateway through which Spirit reveals Itself in yet another way. As we embrace our crucifixion, change our tire, work things out with our spouse, or address the problem of nuclear waste through whatever channels are open to us, we participate in the revelation of that Essence in a most direct and empowering way.

To feel the Essence of nails through flesh, searing sun, and buzzard, and know that this same Essence lives in us as well, is to free ourselves forever from the problem of our crucifixion. Having once recognized Essence everywhere, we can never really identify with circumstance again. There may be occasional lapses of memory, but we will no longer rest easy in illusion.

5

RELINQUISHING SAND CASTLE MENTALITY

As we release our identification with circumstance, it is particularly important to let go of the past. Only in the present moment does the divine plan reveal itself. Only as we pay attention to the movement of Spirit through us in the moment do we realize our place within that plan. Only as we become fully present, do we open ourselves to the living revelation that permeates this world, and allow ourselves to be re-created in the image of the etheric blueprint that underlies our existence. In becoming fully present, we have nothing to lose but the cast-off shell of yesterday's melodrama, now devoid of the divine spark that quickened it to life. Ahead of us lies the empowerment of sharpened focus, and an unprecedented opportunity to participate in the building of a new world of numinous vitality. If we would center our attention upon the living revelation at the heart of each precious moment, and heed the call we find there, the old would fall away of its own accord, and the new emerge unobstructed. We would see the perfection of our unique design, and quite naturally take our place within a whole that is transformed through our participation.

Why then, is it so hard to maintain this focus? What is so seductive about our past history that we mistake it for the reality of our existence? How do we so casually forget our godbeing, as we go about the business of accumulating earthly experience? Why do the temporary forms in which we house ourselves appear more real to us than our Eternal Nature?

Perhaps it is the unspoken fear of mortality that diverts our attention. We are all creatures inexorably caught on the shores of time, building our ephemeral dreams on shifting sands. We work feverishly, one ear constantly cocked toward the ticking of the biological clock, one eye keenly trained past wave after wave for the inevitable approach of high tide that dooms our efforts from the start. Yet, we pretend otherwise. We construct rational justifications about the importance of the building that we do. We strive in countless ways to fortify our sandcastles with whatever momentary illusions of permanence, stability, and regularity suit our purpose. We seek buffers of stability to protect us from the endings that we so desperately fear.

Even our religious beliefs can contribute to the fortification of our sandcastles, if we fail to penetrate beyond the language of physical existence in which their true meaning is clothed. The promise of heaven, reincarnation, or whatever other brand of afterlife we hope to come home to, only serves to perpetuate our clinging.

Until we are ready to surrender all that is attainable within time for the timelessness that lies beyond physical form, we will suffer one cataclysmic loss after another. In the end, when mobility within the timeless state is required for our survival, we will find ourselves adrift upon a sea of confusion.

All that occupies us upon this earth - all that has a beginning and ending in time - must be surrendered to the inexorable flow of life itself. Only then can we rediscover the key to immortality that unlocks the door to our true Essence. This is the surrender that all of us must make, sooner or later. If we do not make the choice consciously, life will inevitably press the choice upon us.

In the days to come, we will all be required to let go of our past. The road we have travelled to get to where we are now need not, and indeed, must not define the road we have before us. As we grow in consciousness, Spirit's plan for us also evolves and modifies our purpose to accommodate greater capacity for responsibility, broader range of influence, and more challenging tasks. In this sense, yesterday is only the springboard on which we are empowered to make the leap of faith that our godbeing requires in the present moment. Once having made that leap, our springboard is better left behind, lest it prove a limiting piece of baggage to the rest of our journey.

All that binds us to the past is, in fact, a potentially dangerous link to what is destined to be sacrificed in the rapid flux of planetary transformation.

For this reason, it is wise to distinguish between those forms in which we participate, where the life force is growing lighter, more fluid, and more luminous, and those forms in which our energy is merely trapped by habit, convention or unresolved karmic pattern. There is no more time to linger with what is comfortable, but no longer vital to our growth; no time to ignore the lessons that keep us running around in circles; no time to waste in identification with the passing show of outer forms, role functions, or adopted masks of convenience.

We must learn to extract the essence of each experience through our undivided attention in the moment, and then move on. The essence of each moment contains a vital key, not only to our growth as individuals, but to the part we must inevitably play in the survival and healing of the planet.

To be caught in the past is to miss our cue, and fail to make that contribution to planetary process that only we can make. To be focused in the moment is to make optimum use of what our past experience has taught us, without being limited by unnecessary biases that only add to the confusion.

On one level it is true that our past experience is what makes our present contribution possible. The vitality of character each unique being brings to the whole is derived only through experience, and all such experience is past or passing, even as we identify with it in the moment.

It is not, however, the experience itself that is important, but the inner process, the transformation of being that takes place through experience.

In the moment of experience itself we cannot always know what it is of value that we are being given by Spirit, but we can always pay attention. We can consciously attune ourselves to feelings, to spontaneous insights, to the divine intention at the heart of each experience. Later, as the seeds which have been planted in the moment begin to take root in the soil of our being, and send forth shoots above ground, additional revelation will unfold. In this way, the full meaning of our experience is gradually revealed.

In fact, it is only in the assimilation of the meaning of our experience that true disengagement from the past becomes possible. As long as we fail to realize the truth within our past experience, we fail to be released, and we miss our passage through the present moment. This is not to say that we must leave the present moment to try to recover what our past had to teach us, only that we must be open and receptive to the flowering of the past that is spontaneously revealed in the here and now. As we realize, accept, and integrate this flowering, we free ourselves to disengage from the forms through which the flowering has taken place.

What we sometimes forget in our rush toward the future, is that the past only slips out of the present moment because we fail to stay in touch with what is there to be perceived. Our senses probe only so deep, and go no deeper. Our mental associations crowd upon the newness of the moment and choke it off from the truth it would otherwise reveal. When all that is left is a reflection of our failure to remain open, we lose interest and move on.

Our insatiable attention races off again. It is not that what we leave behind is devoid of further meaning or value to our growth processes, but that we lack the commitment or the patience to extract what is there.

For some the intensity of connection exceeds the capacity of the nervous system to channel light. For others the focus of attention is too unsteady to capture divine subtlety. For still others, mental and emotional rigidity makes dancing to a rhythm that swings between the polarities of life and contradicts itself at every twist and turn, seem too crazy to be safe.

Yet, in the last analysis, every moment of this earth plane existence contains all of life within it. Every life situation, every encounter, every breath is potentially the door to the Center of the Universe, to the Hub of the Wheel, to the Mind of God, were we capable of plumbing to its endless depth. It is only because we can't or won't consider this possibility that our individual, apparently separate lives move on, and we continue to hunger, even as we leave a trail of crumbs behind us.

It is only because life is so ultimately benevolent, that these crumbs are continually gathered together behind us, recombined in new ways by the Master Baker, and placed on the table just around the next bend. It is only because the sacred mystery of endless self-renewal is within our ultimate destiny as human beings to grasp, that the recycled bread of life is always fresh, even though we tend to think we have tasted it before.

As more and more of us move fully into the present moment, and allow our appreciation for the richness of experience to be found there, energy is released for the creation of new forms. These new forms will continue to house the essence of that which the old forms tried to capture, but in a more accessible way.

No longer will experience become enshrined in mere convention, empty ritual, or blind tradition. No longer will the truth of past experience become the unyielding standard by which present truth is measured. No longer will collective forms be assumed or expected to suffice for the channeling of individual process.

Instead, all experience will be valued to the extent that it releases meaning in the moment. Each moment will be recognized as the unique carrier of truth that it is. Form will command respectful identification from its participants only so long as it serves the unfolding process of Spirit.

New forms will create themselves with the energy that is released as we disengage ourselves from what is passing.

These new forms will be as living beings, changing, growing, serving as ever more powerful and efficient channels for Spirit, just as we do. Breathing, ingesting, and releasing in vital symbiotic exchange with the ever-changing pantheon of unique beings that dance together, such forms will no longer constrain the movement of Spirit through this world. They will instead provide an arena in which the full undiluted glory of Spirit can be revealed as a fact of everyday life.

6

THE GRAND RE-MAPPING
OF REALITY

Our response to life in the present moment is often based upon assumptions formed at some point in the past.

The circumstances these assumptions were formed under have long since passed away, but became internalized as mindsets. These mindsets disempower us because they cut us off from the flow of living information that points out our best path forward. Life has moved on, while we remain entranced by perceptions that no longer apply.

Relying on these mindsets for our information, we get into the habit of not perceiving. We become increasingly divorced from reality, and set ourselves up for our own rude awakening. As the rate at which the world of form changes is accelerated, much of what we have taken for granted will change beyond our recognition. The easier we can let go of our mindsets, the easier will be the transition we are being called upon to make.

As we dare to perceive anew in each moment, we will be propelled through the sheer excitement of self-discovery to make our contribution to the grand re-mapping of reality.

The old adage that says there is nothing new under the sun will be proven false, as each of us finds within a piece of the puzzle no one previously knew existed. The world will celebrate a brand new day, and each of us will proclaim that day with unique fervor and unmistakable style. Together we will cast off the old and unveil the new, because we ourselves will be made new through our willingness to perceive afresh in the moment.

The more willing we become to look again where we have previously seen through the eyes of our mindsets, the more astounded we will become at the boundless Creation in which we are privileged to participate. The entire universe will suddenly be revealed as multi-dimensional, richly hued, and endlessly fascinating.

As each of us shares our adventure of discovery, the mindsets and pet illusions of those around us will also shatter. The light of living revelation will cast all stale perception into shadow. This is the supreme service that we perform for each other, as inevitably we all move toward greater honesty as a matter of survival. In gently pointing out to each other where we cling to old perceptions that no longer apply, we express our love as one soul to another. We give each other the gift of a more genuine reality. The more humor, the more imagination, the more good-natured surrender we can bring to this task, the more of a liberation it will be for all of us.

It may be we are caught off guard by our sudden recognition of truth in places we have tried our hardest to deny it. So, let us all laugh at ourselves. We are all caught with cosmic egg on our face. We have all protected ourselves from phantom shadows on the wall. We have all clung to our delusions like drowning rats upon a ghost ship going down. Now that we are willing to look again, however, and step aside from our trances, we grand re-mappers of reality can have a good laugh together, and move on with a more agile, less encumbered step.

Although we can and must go about this business of undoing old perceptions playfully, let us not underestimate the seriousness of our task. The work to be done can also be characterized as a lifting of the veils, perhaps as the stone in front of the tomb of Christ might have been removed in announcement of his resurrection.

No mistake must be made in our interpretation of the remarkable events we are about to witness. It is vitally important for us to understand the economic, political, and socio-cultural rumblings that grow louder day by day in the light of evolving spiritual design. What is happening is not what appears to be happening from the standpoint of our rational mindsets. Nothing within appearances can give a reliable clue to what is really going on. Just because we may feel we have seen it all before does not mean that we are truly seeing what sits before us now. Peering dimly into shadows, it is easy to forget the divine plan continues to unfold right beneath our noses.

So much within our experience is taken for granted.

Much of what we think we understand has, in reality, not yet received our clear attention. So many of the myriad forms evolved upon this earth for divine purpose have been cursorily and arrogantly misjudged because we think we already know what they are about. Anything that does not fit our mindset, our preconceived notion of how this world should be, is subject to our careless destructive folly. We swat out at what we are not willing to understand, the way we swat out at flies that dance around our heads.

Yet, there is a definite price to be paid for the arrogance in which we tout our mindsets as the gospel truth. If we're not willing to wait for each form that enters our life to reveal its own truth in its own time, then we are destined to live among half-truths and distortions. If we're not willing to see that all forms have their place within this world, then we are doomed to be forever incomplete. If we're not willing to chew the bread of our experience completely, and eat with gratitude and wonder all that is given to us, then we may always have more, but we will never be satisfied. If we're not willing to see the old with new eyes, and take responsibility for our part in the endless process of re-Creation, we are destined to be the suffering witnesses of death and decay. When will we learn that it is not the universally celebrated stone but the one that the builders reject that forms the cornerstone of the temple? When will we realize that it is not the untrusting gatekeeper, but the unannounced guest that holds the key to the riddle of life in her heart? During this time of transition, we will all have ample opportunity to be the unannounced guest at our own castle gate, to hold in abeyance the one who already knows all the answers, to let the Fool within bring his missing piece back to the puzzle of our existence.

Do not be deaf to the voice in the shadows that calls you off on some tangential adventure from the depths of your mindsets and routines, for it is here that your senses will come alive. It is here that the Trickster will make her dramatic entrance into your humdrum existence. Ushered in on wings of fanciful imagination, dancing a wild jig of freedom reclaimed, looking directly at you with unabashed eyes, she will draw you into the spell of wonder that surrounds the Cosmic Fool, the web of magic woven by the Perpetually Innocent, the radiance of eternal sunrise upon the Hill of Eyes Washed Clean.

Though the gatekeeper of mindsets that claims to be in charge will try to repel the unwelcome intrusion of One Who Threatens Chaos Unbound, the gypsy blood of your nomadic ancestors will stir within you, and you will hear the cry of a distant pilgrimage. The quest, the eternal longing made manifest in irrational movement toward horizons only dimly sensed, the unscratchable itch to reach beyond for that which is unreachable will gnaw at your mindsets like a wolf in dog's clothing, until you break free once again.

Do not cringe from the dangers of uncertainty that come with not having ready made answers. For in the daring path of fresh perception, inner resources are forged into precise tools, untapped strengths unleashed, and power reclaimed.

When there is no time to think, thoughts are quickened by Spirit. When there is no time to rationalize feeling, feeling flows uncensored from the heart. When there is no time to premeditate action, action moves in accordance with divine plan. When all we can do is make way for the rush of Spirit through us, the way is cleared for all who follow in our wake. Not necessarily rational, not necessarily contained or tamed, not necessarily neatly conformed to accustomed channels of expression, the Trickster within each of us will inevitably take his rightful space within our lives and work the magic of the Unsettled Opening.

Regardless of the psychological veils we attempt to maintain, the truth will wash us clean. How much easier it can be if we choose to look anew, before the onslaught of fresh perception takes us by surprise.

There is a real thirst for experience arising on this planet, a real hunger for the genuine, original transformative event. The trouble is, old maps and mindsets, even those widely popular now, keep us chained to the wall, looking out in the same old tired directions toward the same old tired conclusions. Some of us have grown mighty comfortable, chained to the wall. But for many of us, these chains inevitably grate against flesh that longs to be free.

At best, this chained life is a hallowed, but soporific tradition, passed down from generation to generation by those who feared the unfathomable nature of their own Being. At worst, it becomes a drug that numbs us to the incredible beauty of this life we are blessed to be living.

We are never told that it is possible, much less to our advantage to chuck the old maps and mindsets at each new fork in the road. But there is tremendous creative freedom to be found in daring to question what is otherwise taken for granted. Such freedom is never won by blindly accepting what is passed along by those we feel ought to know, or by allowing our perceptual habits to take precedence over our experience of the moment. Instead we are required to work at the art of fresh perception, and play with those thoughts that have turned to stone.

It is only in our willingness to see, that this life can reveal its secrets. It is only in our daring to look for ourselves that appearances yield to reveal a plan underlying chaos. It is only in our determination to awaken from the cultural mindsets that entrance us that the essence of truth and beauty within our culture can be salvaged for future generations to enjoy.

7

MELTING FROZEN IMAGES

It is hard for many of us to look at life with fresh eyes because often what we see is not what we want to see.

It is hard to feel the vulnerability of our longing to live upon a planet that has been healed, when all around us the hard, cold "facts" of our existence reveal so much suffering and pain. The evidence of our senses often belies the knowledge deep inside that this life is but part of a more cosmic process, and that all is unfolding according to a plan directed by Divine Intelligence. To look around, to see the damage that has been done, to see the apparent groundswell of movement toward the precipice, is to invite despair. To merely dream of a less precarious situation, while everywhere we look the evidence of mounting danger belies our fantasy, is to cut ourselves off from what power we do have to effect significant change.

Yet within the very heart of the bleakest fact of our existence is the seed of pure intention, some small point of light within the Mind of the Creator seeking to reveal itself. Within the heart of our most ethereal vision of how life could be, if only... is the basic substance of real change. Although the gap between what appears to be and what would be if our hearts had their way often seems unbridgeable to the conscious mind, it is in the closing of this gap that the healing of the earth will take place.

The weight of collective thought forms evolving in mass consciousness toward destruction may work against us, in the short run. Ultimately, however, these thought forms will prove to be just as much a part of the divine process as that which we profess to be the obviously preferable alternative. Whatever is being imagined tends to rush toward manifestation with alarming momentum. When we distrust our neighbor, we tend to act in ways that arouse his distrust of us. As we both begin to deal with each other from this place of mistrust, we will inevitably find some excuse to bring our conflict out in to the open, where the mounting tension between us can be released. As it is with individuals, so it is with nations and ideological movements.

Yet, beyond the content of any widely shared image that moves in this way toward manifestation lies the untapped creative potential of feeling energy in the opposite direction. The archetype of the life-death relationship that underlies these images is a powerful catalyst to widespread transformation that works in paradoxical ways. As a great many people respond consciously to tangible images of potential annihilation, they also, simultaneously become more receptive on unconscious levels to images of planetary salvation. Though despair hangs many in the balance between life and death, as death seems to have the evidence upon its side, the will to live that burns at the heart of every living creature, longs more deeply to affirm the sustainable triumph of life. It is this longing within the hearts of increasing numbers everywhere that will ultimately make a difference.

The more fully we can appreciate the true nature of the process that underlies appearances, the more quickly we can dispel the atmosphere of tension and mistrust that currently prevails between those who call themselves enemies. If all "enemies" could realize that they are both essential to an evolutionary process that transcends their differences, much of the tension between them would dissipate. A stronger sense of interconnectedness would begin to emerge through the smoke of battle and transform the nature of the interaction between them. The divisive politics of protection that now characterizes the surface flow of our planetary process would give way to a more cooperative exchange.

Because we refuse to acknowledge the evolutionary process in those we call our enemies, they appear to justify our fears. It is not the real being within the enemy that we fear, but our frozen images of that being. Once we acknowledge our enemies as living, changing, growing organisms, we break the fearful deadlock that rigid perceptions impose upon us. Not only do we then free our enemies to be their highest selves, and empower them to act in accordance with the highest truth available to them in the moment, but we also free ourselves in the same way. The energy that gets released in shifting our focus from frozen images to an evolutionary perspective is more than enough to counterbalance any threat to our survival.

This is the shift in consciousness we are called upon as a planet to make. This is the true challenge the nuclear age has pressed upon us. This is the quantum leap that now becomes possible on a global scale as each of us individually makes the commitment to melt our frozen images. As each of us sees the enemy within ourselves, and ourselves within the enemy, the barriers between us drop.

We both become part of the same evolutionary process. We withdraw our support from whatever serves to perpetuate the illusion of separation and the fear, and turn our attention to the building of bridges to replace the barricades now keeping us apart.

This shift in awareness, accompanied by appropriate action will not only dissipate global tension, but it will also release tremendous amounts of creative energy for planetary healing. It does not take much imagination to see that if the money, time, creative talent, and emotional investment of all those who now work toward protection against the enemy were re-channelled toward conscious participation in the evolutionary process, paradise would quickly be restored.

Yet, it is likely that we will not be moved to heal our perceptions of the enemy until the consequences of our perceptions make such healing imperative. In the meantime, there may or may not be catastrophe and destruction, depending on how quickly we can realize who the enemy really is.

It should be noted that whatever destruction proves necessary will not affect the Essence housed within the forms that are destroyed. It will disrupt the complacency in consciousness that has lead to stagnation in our perceptions of those forms. The seed patterns of all forms remain eternally undefiled on etheric levels, in suspension, as it were, awaiting the revitalization of consciousness that can activate them again according to the full numinosity of their potential. The rebuilding that takes place in the new age will not take place along totally new lines of approach, but according to these timeless etheric patterns seen once again in the light of their undefilable Essence.

It is possible, during this transition period, to begin reactivating these suspended seed patterns through our commitment to see beneath surface appearances. The fallen state is no more real for any of us than our willingness to let go of outmoded forms and see this creation with the eyes of a child, that is to say, in appreciation and without fear or judgement. Beyond these fears and judgements, everything exists as divine intention would have it, as it was in the beginning, and as it shall always be.

We can see our world this way if we are willing to look again at whatever invokes our judgement or our fear. If our heartfelt intention is to connect with the essence of another being, or the object of our fear, or the problem before us, we will find a way. As we make a space for the enemy within our hearts, we will feel her essence as we feel our own. We shall see that the barriers we have established in our minds on the evidence of the differences between us are the barriers between us and paradise restored. We do not need to try to make this restoration happen. We need only look beyond appearances, relinquish fear, and take down the barriers keeping us from our "enemies." There is truly nothing to fear but fear itself.

It is perhaps one of the greatest paradoxes of our time that as the world situation becomes more intense, our survival increasingly depends upon not getting caught up in that intensity. Fearlessness and genuine peace are now the greatest gifts that we can offer to a world that is keyed up to expect imminent catastrophe.

Because we are also part of the great momentum of our shared global melodrama, we must make an effort to stay in that effortless space where we are naturally fearless and peaceful. We must work at retaining our ability to see Essence everywhere, to see this world with the eyes of innocence. Otherwise, we only recreate the enemy in our frozen images in order to deal with mounting inner tension.

With the enemy before us, we grind away at the planetary grinding wheel, and let fly unnecessary and dangerous sparks, enough of which can inundate this world in flame and mass hysteria.

The enemy does not exist, except within our fear. To heal a world bruised and battered in the ongoing battle between enemies, we need first to heal this fear. Where there is no fear, there can be no separation. Where there is no separation, there can be no battle. Where there is no battle, the paradise that seemed to disappear when we became afraid will "miraculously" re-emerge.

Those who would strip the garden of its trees, and mine the earth of its jewels, all in the name of protecting themselves against the enemy, ultimately do battle only with themselves. In their fear, they cut themselves off from the Source of Life, and grow older every day. Those who are willing to see with the eyes of a child, who are willing to see Spirit at the heart of the enemy, melt the frozen images that lock this planet in self-destructive patterns, and bless the garden seed with the liberating touch of Spring.

8

RECLAIMING THE EYES OF INNOCENCE

In the natural movement of life, form constantly evolves to reflect the ever-changing needs of Spirit.

Through the simple willingness to maintain a beginner's mind, the forms through which our lives continually shape themselves change quite naturally in accordance with divine will. It is only as we cling to the comfortable and the familiar out of fear, that the flow of Spirit through us becomes blocked, and we experience the constraint of our own self-imposed limitations.

As we identify with these limitations, we perceive change to be dangerous, and will strive to maintain the relative stability of old forms. We trade our essential innocence for a limited perception plagued by biases and convenient distortions. It is often a blessing we do not recognize when Spirit assumes a form that throws our biases and distortions into question, for we are forced to look again at something we would rather take for granted. Spirit can alternately be loving or harsh, peaceful or aggressive, joyous or sorrowful, harmonious or disruptive, light or dark, depending upon what we need for our awakening.

Spirit, in fact, can be understood to be the balance in all things, the rectifier of unbalanced identification with one side or the other of any reality.

This is so because Spirit is essentially neutral.

Beyond all outer manifestation Spirit is a magnetic vacuum, drawing us all into its unfathomable Core. What exists at this Core cannot be put into words, for it transcends language. To know the Core is to disappear from the realm in which separation is possible. To know the Core is to understand the neutral balance between all polar opposites.

To know the Core is to become identified with Spirit drawing all back unto Itself, and to no longer be fooled by the many contradictory guises that Spirit takes.

Until we know the Core, Spirit will continue to alternately seduce and shock us, drawing us in whatever way best suits Its purpose in the moment. The more identified we are with one extreme or another, the more we will be bounced around between polarities. The more closely we can identify with nothing but the Presence of Spirit, the smoother our lives will flow.

Regardless of what life looks like from the perspective of the melodrama, we are only being drawn to the eye of the storm, to that place of inner neutrality where the separation between this and that ceases to be relevant, where time collapses, and we already are what we aspire to be. In this place and only in this place can we be ordained as servants of divine will. Only where we are willing to see the Essence that lives within each form, do our lives contribute to the emergence of that Essence in the world around us. Only in our innocence do we see how all things are interconnected, how all things serve a divine plan that unfolds beyond the veil of separation. Where we insist upon believing in separation, regardless of how skillfully we can manipulate form, we only wrestle with illusion.

We have all been conditioned to feel that our innocence is a burden, because it prompts us to act in ways that seem to be out of harmony with the prevailing social order. But the prevailing social order is a distortion of the divine intention that gave rise to it in the first place. Only the eyes of innocence can discern the divine intention beneath distortion, and only those outrageous actions that stem from innocence can cut through the distortions that blind whole societies to their essential purpose.

There is nothing in this universe that will not bow to the transformative power of our innocence. Witness the unshakable faith in the power of God that enables Mother Theresa to accomplish the impossible, or the clear intention of the Olympic athlete that sees victory as inevitable in his visualizations and then goes on to win the gold medal as a *fait accompli*.

It is the actions that stem from innocence that mark our unique contribution to the whole, and it is to make this unique contribution that we have taken birth upon this earth. If we cannot dare to be the radical beings that we really are, that contribution will not be made, and the greater whole of which we are part will suffer incompletion.

We function creatively using 10% of our brain capacity only because the freedom contained within the unexplored and unclaimed innocence of the other 90% makes absolute mockery of our cage. It is time to recognize the forbidden fact that the bars in which we house ourselves are bendable, but that business as usual won't bend them. It is only as we become centered within our innocence as a political act of self-assertion against a momentum rooted in fear that our impact upon this world can be felt.

It is no longer justifiable to go about business as usual in a world where business as usual necessitates tacit acceptance of society's distortions. It is time to shift from the goal orientation that society sanctions, and align ourselves with divine intention. It is time to find the center point of balance at the heart of Spirit, and see beyond the illusion of polarity. It is time to reclaim the eyes of innocence. It is time to play at being innocently outrageous and outrageously innocent, so that in our play we might know the healing embrace of the neutral Core.

9

TRADING SMALL IDENTITY FOR ENTRY TO THE MYSTERY

Through the conditioning influence of this culture, we inevitably trade our innocence for the worldly success that comes through accomplishment. We mark our passage with definite milestones that reflect a certain level of achievement, and evolve an identity for ourselves that builds upon all that has come before. According to this standard, the life well-lived is one that shows a significant level of continuity from one phase to the next, and makes a cumulative statement. Ideally, this statement demonstrates an underlying purpose that emerges and clarifies itself over time, so that at the end of a life well-lived, we can say, "This was my contribution."

Yet, for all that has been supposedly accomplished throughout the course of human history, the survival rate of identity seems mighty low. How many of those who lived one hundred years ago are still remembered now for their accomplishments? How many of those who lived a thousand years ago are remembered at all? Who was it who discovered fire? Or the wheel? Or human language? A thousand years from now, who will remember Ronald Reagan? Or Mother Theresa? Or Madonna? If we can look to the evidence of history then, it would seem that with the passage of time, accomplishment becomes divorced from identity. The cumulative momentum of accomplishment remains, and certainly bears its influence upon events that follow, but the significance of whatever identity lies behind accomplishment only fades. Each of us comes to play our part in a drama that swallows our individual life as but a droplet in a mouthful of water.

For all of our apparent accomplishment, in the end, our passage across the screen of time will have been only a nondescript and unrecorded blip, a speck of dust in the eye of God, a momentary twitch in the body of the Planetary Being. For all the sound and fury we bring to our lives, in the end, our achievements are a fading echo upon the wind, blowing hard, but signifying nothing.

And yet, how many of us react to these words as though threatened, or personally affronted? What are the feelings that arise as we contemplate the utter meaninglessness of our proudest moments? Do we protest? Do we deny that this is true? Do we resent the inference? Do we list our accomplishments as evidence that we are an exception to the rule? Do we laugh at the absurdity? Do we cry with defeat? Do we sink into depression? Do we click our heels with delight, and fly into the heart of life with reckless abandon? Do we place our fingers to our mouths and shush the speaker in an attitude of knowing conspiracy? Do we roll over and play dead? Do we sell all of our possessions and hit the road to preach the gospel of apocalypse and doom? Do we join a convent and devote the remainder of our days to selfless service?

Well, chances are, we simply shrug and continue doing what we are already doing. After all, who among us has not at one time or another contemplated her utter insignificance in the overall scheme of things, and chosen to proceed as though she had never really asked the question? For many of us, the whole question of our ultimate significance within the cosmic order has become a moot point. Our awareness rarely extends beyond the circumstances of our own lives, or the daily events of the world around us. And if it does, how often do the implications of our inquiry actually trickle down, and affect the nitty gritty of our day to day existence? Yet, paradoxically, the way we contemplate our insignificance does make a significant difference. If we choose to deny that we have felt the feelings that come with contemplation of insignificance, we fall back into a kind of sleep. We dream a life based upon the building of identity, only to find at our death, that we had only been dreaming.

The blip across the screen of time begins to fade even before it has had its moment. The identity we have struggled all our lives to build is blown away like sand across the beach, even before it has had a chance to anchor itself on solid ground.

If, on the other hand, we allow the contemplation of insignificance to dissolve the identity we have constructed in our dreams, we claim a larger Identity that is not dependent upon circumstances, or achievement, or the particulars of our lives for its validity. In so doing, we free ourselves from the weight of self-importance, and at the same time, allow this larger Identity to create something significant through the vehicle of our Presence, and make a meaningful contribution to our collective passage.

What happens to our small identity as this contribution is made is no longer significant. We may be praised to the skies, and carried upon the shoulders of our winning team to the victory celebration. Or we may be crucified. Because our lives have served to clear a passage for Spirit, and not to gratify our ego in the building of small identity, it is all the same whatever happens to that small identity as Spirit moves through us. The sacrifice has already been made in the initial acceptance of our insignificance. All that follows is the work of Spirit, within the cosmic scheme of things, and the simple shedding of old skin, on the level of human melodrama.

Don Juan called this surrender controlled folly. The yogic traditions called it karma yoga, or seva, doing with devotion, but without attachment to outcome. Other spiritual traditions refer to being in the world, but not of it. Still other traditions refer to the same choice with the well-known phrase, "Before enlightenment, chop wood and carry water. After enlightenment, chop wood and carry water." All of these, and other ways of looking at the same thing, point toward the separation of identity from accomplishment we discussed earlier. The difference is that the separation that comes only with time does nothing to further the evolution of consciousness, while the separation that comes from conscious choice takes consciousness as far as it can go in this human form.

As we cling to our small identity, all that we do with our lives is to block the movement of Spirit through us.

If, on the other hand, we realize *and accept* the futility of attempting to build small identity, we also realize that we are standing on the threshold of a mystery. That mystery is the inscrutable, ultimately unfathomable movement of Spirit through us. It is our gateway beyond the realm of insignificance, for in the heart of that mystery, we abide and endure. That mystery is who we are once we let go of trying to be anybody at all.

Trading small identity for entry to this mystery is no mean feat. In fact, it is the only accomplishment of significance we can ever achieve in human form upon this planet. It is an act of supreme surrender, supreme trust.

All those who have made significant contributions to the evolution of consciousness upon this planet are those who have made this surrender. We remember their names, because we are still focused upon the building of small identities.

But they gave away their names long ago, so that Spirit could move through them unencumbered by smallness. In the giving away, Spirit found the elbow room to create, and Creation was taken yet another step further into the heart of mystery. Through them Spirit took another step toward full incarnation on this planet.

Like water flowing into every crack and crevice, where there is nothing to resist it, Spirit flows into every human form where small identity has been surrendered. As it flows, It creates something the world has never seen before through the human life that gives its movement form. The accomplishments that come from the work of Spirit through us are significant because they contribute to the overall evolution of consciousness within form. The recognition of these accomplishments that may accrue to the individual through whom they are made means nothing. It is not what gets created within the world of form that is important, but the fact that as Creation proceeds, the mystery is revealed even as we stand in awe of its deepening unfathomability.

Small identity has boundaries, is defined by beginnings and endings, comes and goes with no consequence. The mystery, however, is boundless, knows no beginning or ending, and forever reveals itself without losing its capacity to reveal still further. Small identity cannot stand at the threshold of the mystery without facing its own annihilation. Yet, without standing at that threshold, small identity has no basis for existence, in fact, does not exist except in the dreaming mind of fear.

Small identity seeks to accomplish, to build walls against the mystery, to build monuments in denial of its own utter insignificance. Yet, in time, all such accomplishment fades, while only the mystery remains. We marvel at the Great Pyramids, not so much because they mark the epitome of accomplishment, but because their accomplishment is obviously born of mystery. Where is the identity that stands behind their existence? Even if a name could be assigned to the accomplishment, say Toten-Atnep, 15th century BC, in all honesty, it would still be the mystery unfolding.

As it is with the Great Pyramids, so it is with each of our lives. Whatever might be accomplished through them, all that will be left of us, once this body has disintegrated, will be the mark of the mystery we have embraced. The accomplishments of our small identity will fade with the passage of time. The same mystery that gave rise to the miracle of our birth, and sought to infuse our lives with continuing miracles wherever we would let it, will endure.

And if we have been truly successful in the living of our lives, those who come after us will not say, "This was her contribution," but rather, "She lived at the heart of the mystery," and "She allowed Spirit to do great work through her."

10

THE REVELATION OF THE
ETHERIC BLUEPRINT

As human beings, we are naturally biased toward that portion of reality we can encompass within the range of our senses, our memory, and our imagination. Beyond this apparatus of the conscious mind, however, lies a vast uncharted territory, inaccessible by the accustomed highways and byways of rationality, but approachable through our dreams, our meditation, and other altered states of consciousness. The truth is we live within this uncharted territory all the time, just as we live upon the earth, but because the focus of our attention is shaped by our human bias, we limit our identification to what we can see, hear, touch, taste, smell, remember, and imagine. We filter out other information. Occasionally, we have an exceptionally powerful dream, whose immediacy and tangibility intrude upon our waking habits of perception. But more often than not, the gates that separate the prison of our rational domain from the outlands of our consciousness are locked with the coming of the dawn.

Although the connection between realities can never be consciously understood, in its entirety, from within our own system, we can gather revealing information through our dreams and meditative explorations. Gradually, over the course of time, we can begin to piece together a more comprehensive picture. At the very least, we will learn just how much what we call reality is dependent upon the conceptual framework in which perception takes place, and that this framework is within our power to alter.

For increasingly longer periods the gates between dimensions will remain unlocked, and the more adventurous among us will be able to slip back and forth between this familiar reality and unfamiliar co-existent realities, gathering rare and precious bits of information about ourselves and about the structure of the universe. Night-time dreams will start the gates within us swinging, but the momentum will be carried throughout the day by a special mechanism set in motion by the forces of planetary evolution. It is time, say those who guide the evolution of life upon the earth, to realize we are multi-dimensional beings, working toward spiritual self-actualization, and serving significant cosmic functions on other planes, as well as this earthly one with which we identify.

In fact, we have had our being on these other planes long before we were engaged to participate in this experiment on earth, and will continue to have our being on these planes long after the experiment has run its course.

We forget that our stay here is temporary. We forget that what we do here upon the earth through countless lifetimes is only part of our cosmic mission, the vast majority of which will not take place on earth at all. Evolving personalities as vehicles through which Spirit can manifest, and learning to manipulate material substance in service to the designs of Spirit is only part of what We have taken form to learn.

We forget that we are the Creators of this string of beaded earthbound lifetimes we wear around our neck this particular eon of time. We are lost within the blink of an eye. It is time to find our way back, and to place this brief moment of time, these momentary roles, this ephemeral set of life circumstances in proper perspective.

What appears to be happening on the surface of life is a mere shadow of an underlying reality that is far more numinous than appearances can ever reveal. To know this reality we must go beyond the evidence of our senses, and experience the interconnectedness that undercuts all apparent barriers of separation. The divine plan reveals itself not through those conclusions that can be drawn through external observation alone, but also through what can only be known as we move inward toward the radiant Core of our Being.

It is time to correct our rational biases. Earthbound existence is not necessarily the focus of our multi-dimensional purpose, although for some of us, it might be.

Some of us, it is true, will find the realization of our cosmic purpose within the context of this experiment called "descent of Spirit into matter" that we are engaged in on earth. For many of us, however, earth is only a training camp, where we gather and assimilate knowledge obtainable only within physical reality, for application elsewhere.

For many of us, our primary work takes place upon other planes, co-existent with this one, though temporarily forced into the background of our consciousness by the hard brilliance of physical plane realities.

We strain at very real and important lessons, forgetting why we have agreed to learn them in the first place. We forget our experience in other worlds, now stranded in shadows cast by this one. Yet, a part of us does remember, and listens constantly for communication from home base. It is this part of us whose patient wait will be rewarded as we open ourselves to our dreams and whatever waking state messages filter through from these other dimensions.

Not all dreams or intuitions will provide this communication. Some will continue to serve their purpose solely within the context of our earth plane existence, reorienting the attention of our rational consciousness toward that which it needs to attend to.

Other inter-dimensional communications will remind us of who we really are, and explain how our existence here on earth fits into a larger multi-dimensional plan. This communication will not lend itself to ordinary interpretive analysis, for it does not have its roots in rational soil.

It can only be experienced, and allowed to fill us with its other-worldly presence. We can perhaps render this communication more tangible by translating its essence into poetry, art, or song, but we must not begin to think we have captured it, lest we break its fragile spell under the heavy feet of our earthbound trod. If we treat this communication as an inter-dimensional door, moving back and forth through meditative re-entry, gathering and treasuring the ineffable substance we find there, we can begin to anchor it within our consciousness and render more accessible the passageways between dimensions.

Ultimately, our exploration of these other dimensions will reveal the existence of the higher laws that connect these dimensions with ours. The causal relationships worshipped by the scientific world view will ultimately reveal themselves to be governed by more subtle, but more compelling principles not previously accessible to our scrutiny. These higher laws are based, not on physical, chemical, and biological properties, but upon relationship to a preordained order of perfection encoded within the etheric patterns giving rise to physical manifestation.

Understanding of these laws will come primarily unbidden, as an act of grace, as an etheric dispensation, a gift from higher sources. Initial awareness of higher law will often be accompanied by great joy, and a liberating release of anxiety and stress. This is so because these higher laws are all derived from the law of Love, through which all of Creation has been filled with the radiance of Spirit.

In rediscovering these higher laws we contact an ancient memory of how life was in this state of perfection, before our awareness of Spirit was obscured by the outlines of separate form that filled our secondary senses.

Attunement to higher law is simply a matter of shifting our perception back, through the reactivation of this ancient memory, to that state of being where living in the Presence of our Creator becomes our everyday experience.

11

STEPPING STONES OF SAFE PASSAGE

To make this shift in perception, we must make a deliberate effort to slow down, relax our attitude toward accomplishment, and spend more time sensing our environments, both internal and external. Otherwise, we simply plow through our lives, in the manner to which we have become accustomed, and miss the richness of an experience that can only be claimed at an altered pace.

What emerges, as we move into this altered pace, and balance outer activity with listening, will have about it the quality of a dream. The messages we receive within this altered pace will come from a place so deep within the collective unconscious that the normal symbols and languages of waking state consciousness will not adequately convey them. Only through creative activity performed in a restful, centered, meditative state will new symbols emerge to serve as bridges of mediation between our untapped depths of Being and the more accessible world of sensory connection. As we learn to listen and do at the same time, we will tap the creative flow that is necessary to bring the new life we are birthing within the range of our perception. Those who are not willing to listen in this way, will only wind up fighting the life within themselves and mistake the emerging dream for the nightmare it is replacing.

Listening on universal airwaves in the quiet hours, we can eavesdrop on conversations between the various evolutionary forces at work. Provided we can separate these more potent voices from the regular garden variety that normally occupy the mind, these subtle messages will empower us, and begin moving us where we need to be.

With the regular practice of meditation, the flow of ordinary thought gradually slows down, permitting greater clarity, and more thorough assimilation of the lessons that are being learned.

Over time, the inner process becomes a movie in slow motion, stopping occasionally at frames of relative importance. Much new insight and self-understanding can be gained simply by basking in the grace of this spiritual leisure.

What emerges in the course of this slow motion movie can provide a sound basis for reattunement of life focus, for it is generally the most vital of the work still undone that tends to emerge in these moments of altered pace. As we turn our attention toward the focal point of these meditations, the illusions we tend to indulge will expose themselves and the priorities of our life will rearrange themselves according to a higher plan.

Indulging any illusion creates loss of energy, loss of meaning, and loss of time. While this is obvious from the perspective of the slow motion movie, it is not so obvious from the perspective within which we normally conduct our affairs. Most of the time, these illusions are so tightly woven into the fabric of our lives, we scarcely recognize them for what they are, much less find the strength and courage to pry them loose. It is very easy to let go of long-standing illusions, however, while surrendering to the higher truth that the slower pace of the meditative process makes it possible to recognize.

Though the outward flow of events during this time of transition may be marked by unpredictability and in some cases confusion, stepping stones of safe passage will reveal themselves to those who are able to shed their illusions and preconceived notions of how things ought to be, and listen to the truth that emerges in times of altered pace. Certain perspectives, normally concealed innocently within the background context of everyday existence, will emerge from the periphery of consciousness, and reveal themselves to be vital keys to our next step.

Only in the moment, however, will this be true, and opportunity not seized because of self-doubt, ambiguity, fear, or inner conflict, will be opportunity lost. On the other hand, opportunity seized too voraciously by manipulative, inflated, or deluded persons, intent only on self-gain or aggrandizement, will be opportunity suddenly transformed into disaster. Only a middle path, marked by true humility, pure intention, and unquestioning surrender to clearly discerned voices of inner spiritual authority will render these stepping stones a reliable route through the torrents of the time to a more tranquil shore.

For those capable of travelling this middle path, each stepping stone, upon closer examination, will reveal itself to be a truth unfolding where previously only darkness was discerned. Intuitive associations to the stepping stone will suddenly reveal the clear road to meaningful action, and such action taken will in turn clear a space for the next stepping stone to emerge. In this way, those upon the middle path will far outstrip those more hesitant or self-willed, and cut through apparently impossible situations with amazing ease.

Though not everyone will be open or humble enough to perceive these stepping stones, those who are will eventually bring a fresh perspective to others, enabling all to travel accelerated pathways in the times to come. What is being revealed at this time, to those who are ready to understand, is a whole new sense of order and logic. In this new system causality, chronological sequences, and sensory organizations of space are less important than synchronicity; timeless, mythological connections; and relationships of vibrationally sympathetic resonance.

Though many have glimpsed this other possibility for the organization of reality in sporadic and infrequent personal experiences, few have thoroughly assimilated the essential meaning of those experiences. Fewer still have reoriented their lives to reflect their new perceptions. At this time, however, those who have made the most effort in this direction will bring this other possibility for the organization of reality into closer reach for us all.

With this dispensation of perceptual grace, of course, also comes increased responsibility. Most of those who will become the harbingers of the freedoms inherent in the new perceptual order will be those who have felt themselves lost within the competitive shuffle of the old order. In spite of personalities accustomed by habit to dwell in the shadows, these newly energized steppingstone travellers will move into positions of greater prominence and authority within the circles in which they move. Many will find themselves teaching, mostly by example, the mechanics of movement through the new perceptual order to others. In this way, the experience of a few will eventually take its turn upon the evolutionary spiral to become the familiar *modus operandi* of the many.

There will be much information in the days to come specifically related to the reordering of social structures in order to permit increased spiritual communion across old barriers of economic, political, and religious distinction.

Common experiences, perhaps of an outwardly disastrous, or disruptive nature, will bring people together, in spite of superficial differences, and create a stronger sense of the value to be found in interconnectedness and cooperation. At the same time, efforts toward the fearful maintenance of separation will prove disastrously counterproductive. Only where there is that sense of interconnectedness among all life everywhere on earth will the stepping stones of safe passage appear to fill in gaps in the path that would otherwise be too wide to bridge.

As these stepping stones emerge, there will be much reversal in the world of form, much balancing through justice of what has too long suffered inequality and oppression. In the inevitable course of things, what has been full, will begin to empty. What has been empty will begin to fill. He who has been high, will begin to fall.

She who has been low, will begin to climb. All things will taste of their opposites. All beings will experience the polarity of that with which they most closely identify. In this way, rigid definitions will be shattered, and uncertainty will breed fresh perception. An altered pace will prevail. A powerful sense of balance between light and dark, between female and male, between self and other, between all polarities of Spirit will be established and serve as the law of the land. Within that balance we will find a new identity, one that does not depend upon the fluctuation of circumstance or time. Within that balance, all things will be baptized by the mystery, and restored to perpetual innocence.

12

SHEDDING THE ANTHROPOCENTRIC ILLUSION

Until we reach that point of balance, however, ours is likely to be a time of reckoning. Wherever there is a discrepancy between the values that we espouse and the manner in which we live our lives, there will be a strong sense of inner conflict, prompting us toward changes designed to restore our fundamental sense of integrity.

Wherever we speak empty words, mouthing beliefs and attitudes that were passed on to us in some unthinking way, and accepted without question or testing in the laboratory of our own lives, we will be forced to account for our lack of consciousness. Wherever we have not stood firmly rooted in our convictions, but rather allowed the so-called necessities of circumstance to dictate our actions in compromise and self-denial, we will experience the price we have paid. In the end, whatever does not stem from our essential innocence will die the little death of extraneous skin being shed, as we ourselves await rebirth, like the snake, in more streamlined and primal form.

Like the snake, at the core of our being, we are primal creatures, pulsing with the same primordial life that coursed through the veins of our first ancestors, heir to the same unfathomable mysteries. But, enamored of our civilized veneer, we have forgotten these primal origins.

We have lost touch with the mystery. We have allowed our imaginations to atrophy in a world of shallow short-sightedness, and traded the heritage of innocence for a few shiny trinkets of dubious value.

Moving forward under the pretense of civilization, we rape our mother, the Earth, ravage her bones, tear dispassionately at her vital organs, beat our bloodied chests, and call it a good day's work for a good day's pay.

Toting our gilded Bibles, with the name of our beloved Savior hot upon our self-righteous breath, we sanction the slaughter of innocent people around the world, and hone our capacity to annihilate those who do not subscribe to our particular brand of religious, political, or cultural zeal.

Inflated with the rhetoric of high ideals, we justify our abandonment of principle in the turning of the marketplace, and sacrifice our integrity at the altar of economic expediency.

We are people with little sense of shame, and roots that are grounded in fear. We think we are all-powerful, self-created in the image that we would impose on our gods, if we still believed in them. Endowed by our technological prowess with power that we have not yet learned to take responsibility for, we reel across the planet like a reckless drunk, oblivious to the damage we leave in our wake. But for all our bravado, we are every bit as dependent upon the natural rhythms that govern the movement of life upon this planet as were our unwashed heathen ancestors, and in fact, a good deal more vulnerable because we remain so arrogant in our lack of attunement.

It is essential to our survival as a planet that we re-examine our values, and discard those that keep us perpetually out of alignment with planetary rhythms.

Priorities that place humanity outside the web of life, and deny our primal roots are antithetical to our survival as a species, and as a planetary nexus. Ideals that fail to honor the human process as an evolution of consciousness in form keep us doing battle with the unintegrated reflections of our own dark shadows. In our arrogance we fail to see just how short-sighted and limited in scope our strictly human values are, much less how the entire history of human evolution constitutes one small chapter in the full story of the experiment taking place upon this planet.

What we forget in our rush to dominate the knowable universe is that the human condition only reflects a particular phase in the evolution of Spirit through form.

Once we have collectively attained the highest state of being possible within human form, Spirit will continue its evolution toward full manifestation in some new form, where human values and ideals are no longer of any significance.

In the meantime, it is imperative that we shed our arrogance, and assume values and ideals conducive to the survival of our planet. The changes that must be made will never happen as long as we continue to believe that an infinity of abundance exists solely for our exploitation.

From within the anthropocentric illusion that tints our lense, we cannot possibly appreciate the intricacy of the larger web we are part of. Yet without this appreciation, we will inevitably tear that web asunder.

The necessary change in perspective is being facilitated now, however, by new information recently coming to us from sources beyond the human sphere. Attempts at communication with dolphins and other species, as well as work with plant devas and elementals, have begun to refute the myth of the superiority of human intelligence. Satellite photos of the whole earth have spawned theories that recognize the earth to a living organism independent of its inhabitants. These theories challenge prevailing notions of materialism and the lack of consciousness within so-called inanimate matter. Mounting evidence, both of a scientific nature, and as revealed through channeled information points toward the reality of extraterrestrial life, and consequently the relative uniqueness of humanity. Mystical experiences of unity and interconnectedness, previously available only to enlightened masters and adepts are now increasingly widespread.

This information, designed to attune us more precisely to our essence and our purpose here on earth, is now being assimilated by sensitive individuals everywhere. Eventually this information will be employed in the evolution of social forms better suited to the expression of Spirit, the sustainability of planetary life support systems, and individual attunement to planetary rhythms. Such forms will simultaneously enhance the freedom of individuals to be themselves and the ease with which individuals may naturally gravitate toward cooperation for the good of the whole planet.

As the social forms in which we function change to reflect the collective evolution of our consciousness, old values and ideals based on fear and territorial imperatives will safely fall away. As our capacity for love, obedience to the voice of wisdom within, and centered, compassionate action evolve, we require less protection from each other, and from the higher vibrational voltage now pervading this planetary atmosphere. We are rapidly approaching the time when the full force of this higher vibrational voltage may be experienced without fear of psychic overload. As this happens, intermediary values and ideals that have heretofore governed the flow of energy through our social, economic, and political institutions, and our cultural activities, will give way to values and ideals reflective of a new horizon in human functioning.

There will be tremendous pressure, for example, toward the more conscious use and redirection of material resources. Many of those who have money are now beginning to question the use of their money by banking institutions and even by the government. More sensitivity to the needs of the planet and of all its peoples is needed. Beginning with a response to the continental famine in Africa, and continuing through efforts for relief of every kind, collective humanitarian action to raise money for those in need have begun to mark a new a standard in group compassion. In the meantime, an imbalanced budget, volatile stock and money markets, the world's largest trade deficit, and the increasing presence of disenfrachised farmers, unemployed steelworkers, refugees from other collapsed industries, and homeless people throughout the cities of the world render the necessity for change obvious to all but the most callous observer.

Money, of course, is not the root of the problem, for money is only a medium of exchange, that when used consciously, can facilitate creativity on a scale not possible without it. Nor can any one system of economic approach, whether captialistic or communistic, shoulder solitary blame, for each has its faults and trade-offs. It is not the currency itself or the political context in which money is spent that creates the most fundamental problems, but the underlying values which determine where resources are directed.

When the yearly allowance of a wealthy child of twelve in this country could pay the entire annual salary of a Bolivian tinworker with a family of four, one must question the practices of conspicuous consumption that have rendered much of the world hostage to Western greed. When the cost of one ICBM would feed countless thousands of hungry children, one must question the priorities we have allowed to govern our economic system. The underside of the good life is simply too prevalent to allow us the luxury of pretending we have a system that works, however superior it might be to some other system. It would be simplistic and unfair to equate the accumulation of wealth with culpability for poverty, but, in a world where interconnectedness is the prevailing paradigm, the possession of wealth and privilege will necessarily entail greater responsibility for their conscious use on behalf of the common good.

There is certainly room in this world for the tenets of prosperity consciousness and self-empowerment now so widely accepted in New Age circles to filter into segments of society where longstanding lack and deprivation have generated cultural mindsets of despair. There is also room for charity, and for a concerted effort by those who are prosperous to find ways to help the less fortunate to change their situations. Self-empowerment is a realization that needs to be shared. In a world governed by the law of interconnectedness, every act of giving refreshes the common trough from which we all drink.

Wherever another is awakened to her own potential, and given the space to actualize her creativity, she will then be able to help others to see what they can do, and the benefits multiply rapidly. In the end, regardless of what may or may not happen to an economy based upon the exchange of money, the willingness to share and to extend the awareness of the possibility of self-empowerment to others is crucial. What one gains does not come at the expense of anyone else, but simply adds to what is being utilized out of the infinite potential around us. Inevitably the realization that through such sharing all gain will become the foundation of a society more condusive to the flow of Spirit through form.

This is not to say that these changes within our culture will not be without resistance. In fact, as many within the culture refuse to hear the new information which has been and is being given, old values and ideals may maintain a powerful hold for some time. Those who live in fear of inevitable change will cling to their control with amazing tenacity. Yet, in the end, the resistance of these people will only serve to create the very psychic pressure necessary to their transformation. Just as coal may become diamond in the heat and pressure of the earth, even the heart hardened by fear and resistance to change will become purified in the cauldron of higher vibrational voltage.

Many basically sincere and conscientious individuals, who seek to do good, but as yet lack the awareness to understand the changes earth is now subject to, will nonetheless become powerful channels of higher vibrational energies. It should in no way be assumed that those who adapt most easily to the changes will be best equipped to take on roles of leadership in the days to come. In many cases, quite the opposite will be true, as many of the new functions necessary to the further evolution of Spirit through form require a quality of strength and endurance only to be fashioned through initial resistance to external change.

In any case, we may rest assured that the collective transformation of human consciousness is well under way, and regardless of what we do or don't do, we can only play our part in its eventual and inevitable success. There is no stopping the inexorable flow of Spirit toward more enlightened manifestation in form. As a species, we can choose to cooperate with this flow, or we can resist.

Either way, in the end, there is no corner of this earthly sphere that these changes will not touch. To the extent that we have valued all of life and arranged our priorities accordingly, we shall find our rightful place within the new order that emerges on the other side.

13

THE PRIMAL ART OF
LETTING GO

In the early days, fresh from our experience of the garden, we were aware of the Presence of the Creator moving through all form. Each form carried its own significance in the revelation of one or another aspect of Divine Being, and played its part in the revelation of a Greater Whole underlying the appearance of separation. Our primal ancestors, devoid of modern technological wonders as they were, nonetheless knew something that we no longer know. They knew instinctively that something endurable and real dwells beneath the surface panorama of life, death, and perpetual rebirth. They knew how to live in that state of humility, reverence, and openness to the spiritual wonder of experience from which all true power stems. They knew how to participate in the ongoing miracle of Creation. In fact, they did not know how *not* to participate, because they felt no separation from its Source. They knew, though perhaps not in any way that could be explained in scientific or rational terms, how to move with the full power of Holy Spirit behind them.

For all of our pomposity; for all of our inventive genius and daredevil drive to conquer limits; for all of the testimonial baggage the progress of civilization has heaped upon our collective shoulders, we know very little that will truly matter when the life of the earth gets put upon the line. We huff and puff now, but in the moment of reckoning, realizing at last the folly of our self-indulgent ways, panic may well be our final impulsive response.

Yet, through the grace of the One who has bestowed this Creation upon us, such a pitiful scenario need not be our fate. The wisdom of our ancestors is still available to those not too proud to trade our cultural baggage for a lighter, cleaner and more innocent load. What they knew that we have forgotten is that death is as much a part of the creative process as life. They knew the power of letting go, and that death provided compost for new growth.

They were attuned to the whole rhythm of life and death, content to accept the full seasonal cycle of each form.

Contemporary humans have traded this attunement to the rhythm of life and death for a quick and easy ride in an air-conditioned fantasy bubble wrapped in self-reflective glass. We seek to fortify ourselves against death. With all manner of technological wizardry, we seek ever more ingenious ways to perpetuate the illusion of good-life everlasting. Even as the winds of Kali, the destructress, howl about our fantasy bubble, and warp its shatter-proof shield, we refuse to let reality in. Afraid of death, we become the death-dealing aggressors. In this place of fear, it is only a matter of time before we suffocate in our own stewed juices, for there is no enemy but our own refusal to let go. In the end, this refusal may prove to be our nemesis, as what we have become most attached to is stripped away.

As this stripping away proceeds, we will experience the cathartic release of deep emotions. These emotions lie at the heart of our essential vulnerability as mortal beings, and connect us to the primal experience of our own inevitable death. In the passing of all things, death can be seen and felt, and to the extent that we harbor attachment to what passes, we experience suffering and grief.

Yet within this passing lies the the call to remember our Essence, the same numinous reality that we felt at birth, and that we will experience again at our point of passage from this physical plane. What we do with our lives in between will either serve to deepen our awareness, or encrust us within the safe, but stagnant cocoon of illusion. In either case, it cannot refute the fact that we are the numinous reality beckoning to us from both ends of the time spectrum that seems to define our lives. We are the Shining One that lives beyond time. Death is a collapsing of the temporal mirage that hides our essential godbeing, a celebration and return to our true Identity in Spirit.

Though we are inevitably caught in the dream of lesser identity throughout our sojourn here on earth, our mourning for the passage of this identity is not what our life is about. There is a more essential process taking place underneath the appearance of things, which has to do more with learning to see Spirit within both life and death than with maintaining the illusion of permanence.

It is time to take a good look at our lives, to be honest with ourselves about the baggage that we carry, to let go of small identities that keep us from recognizing who we really are. In the end, only what is free to ebb and flow with the breathing of our hearts will survive the turning of the seasons this creation is subject to. All the fortifications we build against the fear of death will be straw in the winds of Kali.

The more easily we can let go of what naturally wants to compost, the less chance there is of panicking in the moment when the corpses of forms we have outgrown are torn from our clutching fingers. The more readily we can accept our essential vulnerability in the turning of the wheel of life, the less shocking it will be when that wheel moves us through the underside of its cycle. The more humbly we can apprentice ourselves as students of the natural rhythms of the earth, the less likely it is that Kali's thumb-crushing of our fantasy bubble will prove a matter of concern.

The letting go that is required of us is a natural consequence of life on this planet, reflected most poignantly in the turning of the seasons. Each autumn, all of life naturally retreats and turns inward. The fruits of the growing season are harvested, and stored for winter, and the fields are plowed under to compost in their cold season dormancy. During winter, there is an enjoyment of the harvest, and digestion of what the year's bounty has brought to our table. New seeds are planted in a warm corner of the house, and allowed to gestate for spring planting. Spring brings the new birth we have planned for and dreamed about through winter. Summer brings the flowering of the seeds that began their journey in darkness on the other side of the cycle.

As it is with the earth, so it is with our lives.

Everything we undertake - every task, every relationship, every involvement that engages our passion - has its seasons, its planting time, its harvest, and its time of dormancy and rest. Attuning ourselves to the natural rhythm of life and death is a simple matter of becoming aware of the rise and fall of our own energies, allowing our creativity to move outward when there is the natural momentum to do so, withdrawing to harvest and digest when we feel satiated or stuck.

THE BIRTH OF THE SHINING ONE

The problem we encounter in this society is that we are oriented toward perpetual spring and summer. Our cultural addiction to the puritan ethic, to an ever expanding Gross National Product, to unrestrained expansion and relentless growth allows no room for the necessary inward cycle of fall and winter. Because we scarcely take the time to digest our experiences, or learn from our mistakes, or settle into a state of restful equilibrium, we create a severe imbalance in the seasonal rhythm of our lives. We deny death its season, and cut the primal roots that depend upon death to feed them.

Where death is not honored for its natural balance within the whole cycle of life, death turns ugly and claims its due in ways that sap the strength and creativity normally available during the lighter seasons of the cycle.

We may set the best of our intentions toward unlimited growth, but where death is not included in our plans, he becomes the cunning saboteur. He stalks our brightest vision for the future in the form of insidious local wars with no end in sight, AIDS and other diseases for which no cure has yet been found, toxic waste that no amount of Superfund money can exorcise, and the spectre of chemical and nuclear disasters capable of quietly choking the environment for hundreds of thousands of years. Although the technology of limitless expansion is often touted as the answer to every conceivable human ill, it often creates more problems than it solves. This is not to say that technologically oriented solutions cannot work, but where technology is not harnessed to a conscious recognition of natural limits, we are too often forced to witness just how self-defeating, and dangerous our pompous claims of technological mastery can be.

For those who still prefer the technological quick fix to the more sustainable process of reattunement, rude awakenings are in store. To those able to make room in their lives for the natural withdrawal of death, and compost the past to which they have been clinging out of fear, the laughter hidden in the winds of Kali can be heard. For those who have learned the primal art of letting go, this laughter will serve to liberate, not extinguish, all that is cherished within this earthly form.

14

MOVING BEYOND
APOCALYPSE

As the seasons turn, and much of green life upon the earth completes its yearly cycle, a parallel completion takes place within the hearts and minds of earth's human inhabitants. The remembrance of mortality that autumn has the power to evoke is especially strong these days for anyone sensitive to the suffering of the earth, as the larger cycle of planetary evolution also moves into a season that feels very much like autumn.

We hustle, we bustle, we do what we do, we plan, we dream, we step forward, all apparently as usual, but also now with a strong, perhaps somewhat ill-defined feeling that something essential within our lives is irrevocably changing. A movement toward apocalypse is in the air.

Regardless of how consciously we acknowledge this possibility, how willing we are to face our fears, few of us can deny the presence of death among us. On the surface of things, business proceeds as usual, but hardly a day goes by that we do not read of some new environmental catastrophe, some new deadly miscalculation by the technological wizards supposed to be working on our behalf. We may skip through our daily lives, blithely assuming that we are immune from whatever damage might be wrought, but secretly we cross our fingers and our toes to keep the bogeyman at bay.

Regardless of how we distance ourselves psychologically from the news of increasing damage to our planetary life support systems, on some level of our being, we are responding to the imminence of apocalypse. Who can deny that this world we love and cherish is being irrevocably altered by human manipulation? Who knows what the long-range consequences of our short-sighted actions will be? Who can afford to sit and do nothing while all around us the Earth Mother cries out for our help? Beyond whatever actions we might be prompted to take, however, we should also know and affirm with conviction, that the deepest Essence of all that we are, all that we can treasure from the depths of our souls, all we can ever aspire toward in our perpetual movement toward the realization of our own godbeing will endure. This Essence will emerge intact through whatever storms might ravage the external dimensions of our familiar reality.

In fact, not only will the most essential manifestations of Spirit survive, but they will flourish, quickened to vibrant life against a background of death, the passage of all that has outlived its usefulness to Spirit, the inevitable falling of autumn leaves in the great cycle of planetary change.

Despite this guarantee that is inherent within our covenant with Spirit, it is important that we all get in touch with our deepest feelings regarding what have been called the last days of this planet. At some point, it may still prove necessary to let go of all we cherish within the world of form. To contemplate this letting go will not be easy for most people, as the feelings touched in doing so are likely to be some of the deepest and most moving we are capable of experiencing. It will be easy to procrastinate, deny the value, necessity, or timeliness of working with ourselves in this way. It will be more comfortable to justify our optimism in the face of unpleasant evidence, just as it is easy to mistake the true intentions of nature in the colorful display of autumn and the balmy days of Indian summer.

The sooner we are able to move through our deepest sense of grief at the death of planet Earth, however, the sooner we can surrender ourselves to Spirit as agents of divine will, and assume our ultimate role in the cosmic melodrama. Even if apocalyptic destruction is not the ultimate transition we all sense is coming, squarely and honestly facing that possibility, accepting it, transmuting the energy of fear we have invested in it, and releasing it, is an important step all of us must take. Doing so, we lighten the vibrational atmosphere in which all struggle to survive.

Knowing that all scenarios, including this one, are hopelessly inadequate to describe the inscrutable movement of Spirit toward Its own realization, we can deeply honor our connection to this earth, but go about our business with less attachment. Never will creative inspiration come more sharply and succinctly than to the mind free from clinging to the end products of the creative process. Never will appreciation for the exquisite beauty of Creation come with greater joy or deeper gratitude than to the heart prepared to accept the possibility that this moment is all there is.

Never will opportunity for self-realization abound with greater profusion than to the soul no longer identified with the forms it continues to play in and through. Never will life be lived so preciously than to those willing and able to let go of all that currently defines that life and face a radically different future with patience, courage, strength, serenity, and gentle good humor.

Whether or not we accept the inevitability of apocalypse, the apocalyptic possibility is a factor we must reckon with. It colors our perceptions, our thoughts, our feelings, and our actions, through our connection to mass consciousness, if through no other channel. To move forward, toward however wonderful a future we can affirm for ourselves and for the planet without first allowing our primal connection to the apocalyptic possibility to transform us, is to move unconsciously toward apocalypse.

To consciously move through apocalypse on an individual basis, and then move forward, is to contribute toward the possibility of a post-apocalyptic future.

Regardless of what we think we are doing at this time, whether it appears we are part of the battle, or part of the creative outworking of the new world order, all that is happening in actuality is the relentless movement of time toward the point in human history when a greater purpose for the planet as a whole can be revealed. What has appeared thus far, from a human perspective, to be a war-ravaged process, leaving millions dead by violence, etching and re-etching national boundaries in blood, and moving the entire planet inexorably toward the brink of global catastrophe, has only been the outer form through which a far greater process has taken place.

From a cosmic perspective, an entire planetary complex of interpenetrating dimensions is living for that moment in time when its identity as a single agent of divine purpose can be revealed. Although from within our anthropomorphic bias, we often act as though the planetary melodrama depends entirely upon the actions of human beings, we are not alone in this process. Angels charged with a mission of facilitating vibrational attunement, devas responsible for the evolution of various life forms, extraterrestrial guardians and mentors, and other unseen and unknown realms of beings all have their vested interest in the success of this experiment we conduct on earth. The day for a more conscious recognition of this truth is coming, but because, in general, we are still so enamored of the forms we momentarily inhabit, that day will not likely come without some further preparation.

Just as a sculptor, faced with a rectangular block of granite, must make some radical blows at first with her hammer and chisel to draw forth her vision, so too must the Sculptor of the Form for this Planetary Being make some radical changes among the various terrestrial forms with which she works. And so, too, just as a sculptor eventually gets to the point when the entire process becomes a more sensitive and delicate operation, the tumult of war and international strife will also subside when the Planetary Sculptor reaches that level of refinement in her work upon this planet.

Upon us who are now working for planetary awakening, the Planetary Sculptor has already made some radical changes. Hammer and chisel are giving way to more delicate tools better suited to our further refinement. While on the more external levels of our being, our existence is seemingly threatened by the battles that rage around us, we can rest assured that because of the work we are doing, the threat of annihilation has begun to subside.

All that has been chosen by the Planetary Sculptor to embody and reflect the glory of a new divine order upon this earth, has already been guaranteed passage to the new world. We can, if we make the conscious effort, assimilate the destructive energies that rage around us now, transmute them in the light of what is already guaranteed survival within us, and breathe back peace into the world. In this historical moment, we can actually guarantee the survival of the earth. Knowing that what is truly of the Spirit cannot be destroyed, but only revealed through increasingly wondrous dimensions of its splendor, we will find the courage to call a halt to our collective madness. In the stillness that ensues, a turning point will be realized.

15

CLAIMING THE FREEDOM
OF THE CHRIST SPIRIT
WITHIN

Those of us who can sense this turning point close at hand, have work to do. As the Planetary Sculptor chisels away our attachments, our doubts, our fears, and our illusions, our godbeing begins to emerge. Though we may be awkward at first in the exercise of our transformational powers, the grace we pour out upon the wounds of this world will flow easier with practice. Though we may initially marvel at the truth put into our mouths, we will soon wield the magical power of words the way we now wield swords. We may stand in awe of the first miracles that take place through us, but we will inevitably come to know these miracles as our daily bread. The blind will see; the lame will walk; the fearful will open up their hearts. All these things will we do, and more.

As we surrender ourselves as channels through which Spirit might do Its work, we will experience an electrifying power coursing through our nervous system. This is the power of Divine Being operating through the thinnest of veils, supplementing our personal capacities with power ordinarily beyond our reach, jettisoning us toward that exhilarating state where we are but agents for a spectacular coup of transformation and reversal.

Through the intermediate stages, there will take place within our bosom powerful and at times tumultuous struggles for balance between contradictory aspects of our nature.

Whatever has not yet been integrated into the whole fabric of our being will emerge as distorted and caricaturized so that we may proceed with diligence toward self-change.

Whatever blocks the free flow of Spirit through us will be expelled. Voices that still whisper of considerations tangential to our purpose will be drowned beneath the sound of the One Pure Tone calling us forward. We will be changed beyond our own recognition, irrevocably altered at an exhausting pace, purified and empowered. There is no time to waste. Our moment of truth is close at hand, and good agents of divine will are still not easily come by.

Our movement through this physical plane will soon be more consciously determined by our function as channels of divine grace. Looking past the level of surface turbulence, and incomprehensible change, we must learn to trust in the existence of a divine plan, and stake our lives upon it.

Where we are locked in fear, self-pity or doubt, we will have our greatest difficulties. Where we can identify, in our hearts, with the tremendous groundswell of movement that exists everywhere toward the positive transformation of earth plane reality, we will delight in the amazing perfection of divine process. We will take our place among others also ready to serve, and move together in the redemption of the earth. While those who look to externals for their security will have their lives scrambled, those who have learned to find their security inside, and are willing to give more than they take, will prosper.

It will soon be up to those who do the work of Spirit to carry the banner of civilization, for the scrambling that occurs in the lives of those who cling to form will cause much disorientation. In some unyielding quarters of tenacious self-will, the release of Spirit through form may appear more violent. Where fear and paranoia are entrenched, passage on the earth plane may temporarily become dangerous.

Equally powerful, however, will be the attunement of loving souls to one another and to the Source of Love. Even amidst the confusion and the darkness, this positive attunement will open doors, manifest bridges, and light difficult passageways for those consciously aligning themselves toward planetary service. Those who permit the Planetary Sculptor Her finest hour, will be protected through all catastrophe.

To experience this protection, meditate on Spirit as pulsating Light within you, radiating from the deepest Core of your Being, from that quiet place in your very heart of hearts - radiating out in soft undulating waves of healing warmth and refreshment. Let this healing Light shine out into the world, first as a gentle blessing to your loved ones, then as a steady statement of Presence and Glory to everyone you touch.

CLAIMING THE FREEDOM OF THE CHRIST SPIRIT WITHIN

The Christ is here now, in you, through you, waiting to lift this planet from the jaws of destruction. You can begin your avatarship here and now, if you choose. The energy of Christ's boundless Love is available, and will surround you with a cloak of guaranteed protection as you go about Your work. Do not pause to consider the endless parade of forms it temporarily behooves You to function through.

Focus instead upon the Light that permeates all form. Let this Light shine through you as a beacon of hope and healing to those who have not yet found their feet in this time of rapid change. Hide no longer beneath the dust the Planetary Sculptor has yet to brush off your shoulders. For this Light is who You are, and your Essential Gift to the world of form You have come to liberate with Your touch.

16

RETAMING THE TRICKSTER

To the extent that you are able to identify with this Light that moves inside of you, rather than the forms through which you move, you become the avatar you were placed upon this earth to be. The human experiment begins and ends with each of us striving to claim our essential freedom, for each of us offers something to the world that has never before been actually experienced, and may never again be possible on the face of this earth. If we choose to hide from this challenge within the comfortable identities that society offers us as options, the human experiment fails because one essential part of the whole is missing. If, on the other hand, we are able to rise above the seduction, and recognize just how much of our culture is constructed as a dike against the floodtide of inevitable change, we can move the human experiment toward resolution and salvation.

What we do from within such an awakened state will often be seen as revolutionary or subversive from within the sleeping culture as a whole. But those (and there are many) now caught within that borderland between sleep and the awakened state are likely to be nudged across the threshold through our Presence in their lives. This is the process we have set about together, but each of us must undergo alone.

No one can do for us what we alone have come here to do, and none of us can realize the full flowering of consciousness in form until each of us consciously claims our pioneering part.

Claiming this part does not mean uprooting ourselves, quitting our jobs, abandoning our homes and families, and taking to the open road with missionary zeal. We need not force the changes we require to release the passion that will drive our pioneering spirit out into the world. We need only attune ourselves to that passion, and allow what our passion burns away to pass from our lives in its own time, of its own accord.

Where our passion encounters our more passive attachments, we need only realize our mourning is just the release of creative energy bound in outworn forms that now cry for liberation. Where our passion encounters the fear of others clinging to their sleep, or to the sleeping culture as a whole, we need only forgive ourselves for the momentary disruption we cannot help but bring to the lives of others.

I say "only", some of you are thinking, as though these were easy shifts in perception or attitude to make. But the truth of the matter is that passion burns its own pathway through the jungle of emotional ambivalence and human weakness. Passion is not afraid of death, but rather knows that death is a faithful ally with machete in hand, ready to clear away the overgrowth that makes detour necessary and fosters despair. True passion is not diminished or extinguished through the passing of form, but empowered with the additional boost of old energy released for new initiative.

Ultimately, true passion, as I am speaking of it here, is the original passion of divine intent. This passion arises as the natural radiance of the Shining One within. It is Spirit's excitement about our being here to do inspired work. It is the breath of life that propelled us on this journey into the sticky realms of physical manifestation and the promise of our redemption from attachment to form.

As pioneers from the realm of Pure Being we were sent here to conduct an experiment, to infuse matter with consciousness and to witness the flowering of a watery rock hurling through space. We were not meant to chain ourselves to the rock, or lose ourselves within the matter that has waited for our touch. The passion that each of us was given when we came is both the tool we need to complete our mission, and the vehicle of our escape, when the job we came to do is done.

Ultimately all paths through this physical plane lead to the same glorious reunion with the Source of Being. In this cosmic sense, all paths are the same. It does not matter, from this perspective, which path we follow. Because this physical plane existence seems to separate us from each other and from our Creator, however, we are compelled to follow one path or another. The passion that burns within our heart naturally compels us, because through this passion the heart instinctively knows the quickest way to the reunion we seek.

Because the heart functions in a realm where space and time do not exist, its path tends to lead us as the crow would fly, taking little account of the fact that on the ground, where we earthbound creatures must travel, there are often hills, mountains, rivers, canyons, and thickets to negotiate. Thus, in following the general directions set in the longing of the heart, it becomes necessary to employ a second agent. The special skill of this agent lies in analyzing terrain, judging distance from one horizon to the next, determining the best way over, under, through, or around whatever obstacles we encounter along the path, and keeping track of time. With one eye attuned to the rising and setting of the Sun, and the other on the lookout for suitable encampments as each day of the journey draws to its natural close, this second agent maps out the best route for us to take as we follow the promptings of our heart.

This second agent is, of course, the mind.

As long as the heart and the mind are clear about their natural functions, the body will carry the precious drop of Spirit it was created to transport, with grace and rhythmical beauty, over hill, mountain, river, and thicket to the Infinite Ocean, where the Source of All Being waits with tender patience for our arrival. Were the heart and mind left to their own devices, neither would ever want to usurp the domain of the other, nor assume a function not its own, and the smooth journey of the body would be guaranteed. In the natural balance of things, the passion burning within the heart ignites the mind as well, and inspires it toward undeviating loyalty in its service.

But there is a third agent housed within the body, representing God's playful side, that delights in making both heart and mind dizzy with its antics. It was originally given us to help relieve the burden of a long, arduous journey by a Creator who knew we would need regeneration along the way. This third agent was endowed from the start with free imagination, will, and steady memory of divine intention. Soon it became so enraptured with its gift of free imagination, however, that it virtually forgot about the other two, developed an acute imbalance, and began to suffer from delusions. It began to imagine that physical plane creation was the source for the light it reflected from its Creator.

It called to the heart, flying straight and true, high overhead, and pointed to the shiny specks of crystal in the rocks on the ground, the sunlight flickering among the leaves, and other delights of earthbound magic. In its eloquence, it convinced the heart to dive down and explore.

Once grounded, of course, the heart got lost, and began to despair of the hills, mountains, rivers, and thickets it now had to negotiate.

All the while, this third agent was whispering in the ear of the mind from the highest mountain peak nearby, provoking it to look around and survey the kingdom of infinite possibility. The mind, reeling in the drunken ecstasy of choice, quickly lost its discrimination, and stumbled off in what appeared from its giddy new perspective to be the most enticing direction, forgetting momentarily the heart it had once faithfully sought to follow. As the mind and heart were stretched in opposite directions, the bond of passion that gave them their power as an integrated unit fell into the bottomless chasm of apathy and despair.

This third agent, or Trickster, we shall call it, got away with its tricks for quite some time, as it does to this day, again and again, with all of us. After awhile, however, the mind and the heart get wise to the Trickster's ploy. The mind becomes determined not to succumb any longer to the Trickster's temptations, and in this determination, reminds the Trickster of its second gift of will. The heart begins to remember its Beloved, even in its snare of earthbound enticement, and in this newly rekindled longing, reminds the Trickster of its third gift of steady memory of divine intention.

As the Trickster begins to remember these other gifts it was given by the Creator, it also returns to a state of balance and the resumption of its original function. Using its creative imagination, it now teaches the heart the poetry of holy flight, calling it sweetly on with gladness and joy, gratitude and appreciation. Meanwhile, it also teaches the mind the magic of natural law, strengthening it with resourcefulness and affirmative attitudes. Thus tamed by mind and heart, the Trickster becomes the agent of accelerated motion toward divine reunion, and the steward of the passion that gives this life its color and vitality.

With the sly wisdom of the partially reformed thief, the Trickster challenges each of us to claim that pioneering spirit we were born with, and play our unique part within the greater plan we have come on earth to manifest. It is up to us to teach this Trickster its rightful place within the whole, so that it will serve us as we serve the greater plan.

17

THE TESTING OF
ALLEGIANCE TO DIVINE
INTENTION

At the heart of each passion lies a divine intention burning with irrepressible will toward manifestation. The entire movement of life through the realm of form can, in fact, be seen as evidence of a greater, planetary will in operation. Though we can just as easily see this life as a product of our own creation, it is time to become aware of the planetary will underneath the flow of external events, and to consciously commit ourselves to cooperation with its intent. In this way, we move beyond powerlessness and wishful thinking toward significant change. Our commitment to the actualization of planetary will becomes the fuel planetary transformation is propelled by.

Before we can fully align our creative passion with the planetary will, we must expect to endure a few tests of integrity along the way. That is to say, those of us wishing to become more conscious of our place within the larger process, must first demonstrate what we have to offer through the strength of our commitment to ourselves. In our faithfulness to our own most sacred ideals; in our relationships to intimates, family, and friends; in our chosen channels of work and service; in our current sensing of our spiritual path; and in every other area of life, we shall be thoroughly tested. Unannounced and with great cunning, the hand of testing will come, probing with uncanny intuition, to uncover doubts and ambiguities, conflicts within the heart, weaknesses of intent. Old patterns of self-denial, self-sabotage, and self-incrimination will be drawn forth to be squarely faced, dealt with, and transcended. The tests will not be easy, but they will ultimately ensure our capacity to handle the higher vibrational frequencies we shall be required to handle.

THE BIRTH OF THE SHINING ONE

Service to a plan that extends far beyond the range of our personal lives will demand more than we have perhaps been accustomed to giving.

A quantum leap in consciousness is possible for us all at this time, but the leap that we actually take will be commensurate with our commitment to the divine intention that gave rise to our birth. Our perseverance toward the actualization of this intention has been the test of our worthiness to encompass higher levels of functioning and cosmic responsibility. To the extent that we have honored our commitments to ourselves and the voice of the divine within, we have become fertile ground for the implantation of new vision, and will soon find ourselves charged with a more conscious mission.

To the extent that we have abandoned our allegiance to divine purpose, we will experience abandonment in these days of planetary transition. In truth there is no such thing as abandonment, for regardless of how long and winding the path, we all eventually return in triumph to the Source of our Being. Yet those who wander aimlessly along the way will undoubtedly lose the way for a good long while, as our allegiance to the calling of the Light within will be the only compass by which navigation is possible.

As we enter the phase of testing, the longing that we experience through our allegiance to intention will be our catapult into a higher level of consciousness. As we seek to honor this intention, there comes a moment of existential desperation. In this moment, we reach a pivotal point where continuity and security are less important than the promise that lies upon the far shore of the nearest quantum leap of faith. In making that leap, we pass the test before us, and prove our utility within the divine process.

Each of us is being nudged with increasing intensity toward the alignment of our personalities with life purposes chosen long ago. Even before the human species took shape within the mind of the Creator, these purposes were mapped out and given momentum. Later, as human beings began to evolve and differentiate themselves from one another, we began a long, trial-and-error process of identification with one or another of these purposes. Now, gradually growing in our capacity to serve our chosen function, we simultaneously move in consciousness toward surrendering ourselves to become agents of a higher will.

THE TESTING OF ALLEGIANCE TO DIVINE INTENTION

From time to time, in the course of human history, individuals have managed to take the necessary leap in consciousness to embrace the vision of their purpose in absolute clarity and attunement. Such individuals grace the pages of our historical accounts with the light of their own immortality, although the words and deeds of many more of them have never been recorded.

For the majority of evolving souls, however, the leap in consciousness has yet to be made. And even though inspiration abounds in those who have made the quantum leap before us, the leap is qualitatively different for each of us, and consequently no less difficult than the first ever made.

Nonetheless, during this time of planetary transition, many more of us will be moved in creative desperation to make this leap. The more of us that hold back in fear, laziness, or some false sense of unworthiness, the more difficult the transition will be. The more of us that can willingly surrender to the transpersonal energies moving through this planetary sphere, the easier the process becomes for us all.

Despite occasional pockets of misguided resistance, unprecedented numbers of us will come into alignment with the specific functional purpose for which we have incarnated. Our longing to know this purpose will deepen through test after test after test. In the end, however, what will make the difference is not anything that we do or don't do, but a timely and beneficent outpouring of divine grace. Through our commitment to Self, we prove our worthiness to receive this final blessing.

Where the pain of effort has been real, where the yearning has been deep, where our commitment has withstood all testing, an unseen hand will cut the fetters of restraint and limitation. Spirit will surge through us, pulling personality behind It through the vacuum of Its passing. As we pass through this threshold, the form world will reveal its transparency. We will feel a sudden snapping through the illusion of outer continuity, a powerful rush of deep freedom and joy, a falling away of small identities that is dream-like, yet undeniably real.

The godbeings that We are, too long relegated to the lofty peaks of our imagination, will suddenly stare us in the face, as we look each other in the eye.

It may come as a surprise that these godbeings we have all this time aspired to become have sat in waiting for millennia, alive with vitality of their own, patiently drawing us toward them, actively guiding our passage in consciousness to the peaks on which they sat. Even as we were reaching upward with all of our spiritual might, they were reaching downward with unfathomable compassion. Our meeting with them was inevitable, has been since the beginning of "time," and now becomes reality for those of us who can cross the threshold of our own unworthiness. Those of us who have signalled our readiness in the joyously painful stretching we have done, in the tangible depth of our longing, can rejoice that the touch of recognition is upon us.

We are entering a time when nothing will remain as it has appeared to be. The rapid onset of planetary purification is stripping away the veils of illusion with accelerated vigor, because the time has come to see clearly. Throughout the history of human evolution, truth has been easily distorted, allowing us to learn much of value from the repercussions of our mistakes. But the time for learning in this way is now behind us.

We have all been training more or less consciously for a cosmic function our minds could not begin to fathom. We had time. We did what we could. Now the time has come for us to assume those functions, to be the agents of divinity we have been training to be. There is little room any longer for pretending to be "only human." We are on the line. Those of us who have perfected our identification with Essence through all change of outer form, and who have attuned ourself to planetary will, are the midwives of the coming age of illumination. We have prepared ourselves to see light, and so the release of light through all form will be cause for celebration, joy, and upliftment.

Those who have chosen to identify with form, and who insist upon serving only themselves will find themselves afloat upon a desperate sea of instability. One in such a hell might be standing side by side with one caught up in the rapturous enfoldment of the light, from the standpoint of physical appearances, but through the eyes of truth, these two will be separated by a chasm no longer bridgeable by act of human effort.

In the days to come, there will be two paths we can travel: the path of self-aggrandizement, or the path of enlightened self-interest in service to the planet. As we attune ourselves to the divine intention that underlies our birth, and base our actions upon this intention, we simultaneously ensure our own well-being, and make a significant contribution to the evolution of consciousness within the larger scheme of things. It is our commitment to know and honor this divine intention that will be tested and that will mark the level of our usefulness to Spirit. In the end, it is this commitment that will ensure our survival.

18

WALKING THE FINE LINE BETWEEN PIONEERING FOCUS AND SURRENDER TO THE RHYTHM OF THE WHOLE

There is a strong need in this age to join with others of like spirit. Each of us has been experimenting with life, testing our wings, mapping our personal realities as we proceed. Because each of us has a unique contribution to make, we must necessarily walk a solitary path. Yet, as each of us attunes more deeply and with greater focus to our individual purpose, we realize simultaneously our inexorable connectedness to the greater whole. The energy we hold in sacred trust begins to converge with the energy of others holding that same trust, each in a special way. Like so many tributaries flowing independently into the same river, we find the current quickened in the excitement of our blending, and begin responding from a deeper place within to the rhythmical lure of the ocean that marks our common destination.

Yet, as enticing as this movement is, we must remember the personal vision where our convergence finds its grounding. We must walk a fine line between surrender to the collective flow and maintenance of our individual focus, for in the balance between the two lies the sweetness of our merging. To surrender too quickly or unconsciously into communion, we lose the special gift only we can bring to the celebration of our unity. To hold too tightly to the focus that has allowed our special gifts to unfold, we risk failing to find a place for them within the intricate choreography of the greater dance. To step in rhythm with the greater whole, we must find the balance between holding fast and surrender that permits a conscious and deliberate

87

blending. It is toward this coordinated rhythm that the process of planetary evolution is taking us. For some time now, the planetary choreography has been geared toward arranging things so people who hold adjacent pieces of the puzzle would find themselves in close proximity to each other. As this process continues and intensifies, there will be much to share and celebrate.

While it may often prove necessary to walk alone in order to birth the vision that burns within us, there are powerful ways we can participate in each other's quest. Indeed, although the paths we travel can be quite different, what we are learning through our exploration is vitally important to each other.

Those we love can find confirmation in our discovery of ourselves, as we can find confirmation in theirs. Our solutions to life's challenge can open doors where our neighbors face only walls. Our mistakes can help others to avoid much unnecessary suffering. Our joy can rekindle the waning enthusiasm of our travelling companions during times of discouragement or low energy. Ultimately we are here for each other, and only as we work together can we find the long term endurance to play our individual parts within the whole.

For those who have developed a strong sense of personal vision, while at the same time loosening their identification with form, there exists a real opportunity to celebrate with others the universal truth that transcends form altogether. It will be a great joy to witness the flow of spiritual exchange between people of widely diverse temperaments and backgrounds who come together in this way.

As individual mindsets and prejudices are suspended in communion with others willing to do likewise, a mutual revitalization will take place, enabling each of us to express our individuality with augmented power. At the same time, a synergistic creativity transcending all barriers will unite us in higher purpose.

In any group where strong individuals come together, there are bound to be areas of friction and blockages in communication. Such friction can, however, if viewed in the light of commitment to group purpose, serve as a powerful catalyst to the development of group potential. Where interpersonal blockages are approached with mutual desire toward resolution, new levels of communion and group creativity can be attained. In many cases, a quality of relationship can be achieved that perhaps would not be possible were there no issues to be resolved.

Where good relations already exist, a telepathic level of communication can be reached where a single inspirational pulse beats simultaneously within separate bodies and accomplishes separate, but related tasks at once. Such rapport between people working together along the same channel of service will become commonplace, as the new vibrational energies evolving on earth begin to anchor themselves more securely through group work.

It is inevitable that as the process of planetary evolution proceeds through this group work, the egocentric perspective that keeps separate individuals working in isolation and in competition with their neighbors will gradually be abandoned. Artificial barriers will dissolve, and differences in background and style of approach will become the gap through which sparks of innovation fly. Win-lose situations will resolve in win-win possibilities that draw forth the highest potential of all involved. Mistrust will dissipate, and common purposes will emerge to unify focus. Those who formerly allowed their differences to serve as points of contention will work together synergistically for the good of the greater whole, and the spirit of cooperation will waft across the land.

19

THE HEALING BALM OF INTERCONNECTEDNESS

Wherever we find our intentions merging with like-minded others, the chemistry of our interaction can be a potent force for meaningful change in this world. It is no longer enough, however, to simply desire world peace, or an end to hunger and starvation, or the restoration of ecological balance, or any of the other noble goals we might wish for earth and its inhabitants. We must be willing to take direct action in order to bring these things about. We must be willing to get our own lives straight, and work things out with those we previously called our enemies.

Peace is not something that happens between heads of state in Washington and Moscow, but rather a healing of hearts that takes place in our own neighborhoods. Wherever we experience disharmony in our relationships with partners, lovers, friends, our children, our business associates, or our neighbors, we have our opportunity to work toward peace.

Hunger is not something that happens only in the Third World and the back streets of America. Hunger in one form or another is all around us. There are those who do not have enough to eat, and of course, these must be fed, and empowered to feed themselves. But there are so many more in this world who hunger for the warmth of human caring, for someone or something to care about. These too must be fed, and awakened to the unlimited love that pours forth from the godbeing at their Core. Wherever we can feel the pain of human suffering, we are being called to do this feeding and this awakening to the higher truth of self-empowerment.

Nor is ecological disaster something that happens only in some remote rainforest, or distant backwater stream. The habits of consumption we take for granted, the material greed that fails to appreciate or steward the bounty that surrounds us, the impoverishment of spirit that prefers charcoal and chipboard to the mystery and magic of hundred year old trees, all deplete this world of its beauty and its lifeblood. Wherever we blindly consume, or take this world for granted, or disregard the consequences we pass down to future generations, we contribute to the deterioration of a world under stress.

The human species has been on a binge. We have taken for granted the abundance and the majesty of this garden planet we are blessed with. We have trampled through the wildflowers in the drunken reverie of our self-importance.

We have tossed each other over cliff and precipice in fits of disconnectedness. We have slit our own wrists, gazing bleary-eyed at endless horizons that do not exist, except in the plexiglass fantasy bubble we have constructed to protect ourselves from the stalk of death and natural ending.

As each of us begins to reawaken and face the morning after, we have our work cut out for us. Planetary healing is not some lofty, intangible ideal. It is a crucial matter of undoing the damage we ourselves have done, of healing our own lives, our relationships, and the environments in which we live. We need look no further than the suffering we ourselves experience, and the suffering of those around us to find the work we are being called to do.

For those with the capacity to do so, opening to the suffering of humanity will be the quickest avenue to meaningful action. To cry the tears of those unable to cry for themselves; to laugh the laughter of those unable to appreciate the humor of their own folly; to vent the anger of those afraid to refuse oppression; to consume the fears of those trapped by their own attachments; to transform all of this tumultuous, unchannelled, unacknowledged and disrespected energy in the healing silence of our own hearts, is to do a great service to the planet at this time. The actions that stem from this depth of caring will be rooted in interconnectedness, humility and compassion, and feel the full power of Spirit behind them.

This work will necessarily take many forms, but what we must all be about in the days to come is the alleviation of our ignorance. Each of us is a carrier of hard-earned wisdom, and each of us also has our blindness. We are here to apply the healing balm of our understanding to each others' eyes, and draw forth clearer sight. We are here to hold each other in love and compassion, and in that space permit a deeper knowing to emerge. We are here to teach each other, to sit at each others' lotus feet, to remind each other of our godbeing, to encourage that godbeing out into the world, where it is so sadly needed everywhere we look.

The people we are most intimate with in our daily lives are those who are most capable of mirroring the godbeing we carry inside, and illuminating the shadows where godbeing is wont to hide, while we do the same for them. It is no accident that we have opened ourselves in trust to those we call our most intimate companions on this journey, and no mistake that we share the lives we do with these companions.

We are all in the best position to heal the wounds and dispel the darkness for those we love most dearly. And as this age of awakening progresses, we shall all begin to see that our greatest teachers are those who touch our lives most closely. We need not look outside of our lives for that special teacher, one in the business of collecting disciples or conscious of a particular teaching mission. Much closer to home than the exotic or the esoteric, is everything we need to know, and more. Wherever we are willing to hold no secrets from each other, forgive each other our trespasses, and see each other in holy innocence, we are awakened to a deeper remembering, and a powerful healing takes place. We remember the agreement we made with each other before we descended onto this earth plane. We remember the collective vision that inspired us to leave our nesting place in Spirit to brave the dangers of this material world. We instinctively move in harmony with our essential human purpose.

When we empty ourselves of all that keeps us separate, that emptiness becomes the lifeblood of the Greater Self we share, and begins to flow with new vitality. As this Greater Self then comes alive, a planetary culture emerges through which we are once again empowered to live in harmony with the divine plan we were all created to serve.

Before such a planetary culture can emerge, however, we must learn the exercise of compassion toward ourselves and toward all those who have done us wrong. We must come to understand, through our compassion and our forgiveness, that all mistakes are vehicles for realignment to the will of Spirit. The fact that mistakes are inevitably made by all of us is unimportant. What is important is the learning that takes place through them. Sometimes the very worst mistakes are the best learning opportunities.

When we focus on each others' faults, when we allow our shortcomings to be more real for each other than the godbeing striving to realize itself through us, we generate an atmosphere of inhibition and repression in which it is impossible to learn or grow. When we focus on the learning that takes place through our actions, and allow others the space to learn from their actions, we feed each other and care for each other in a most fundamental way. We need to look past our apparent imperfections and see the growth taking place, see the evolution of consciousness that permits Spirit to reveal Itself, see Spirit Itself dissolving all barriers of separation, as It teaches us of our essential wholeness, our interconnectedness, and our unity.

If it is only our human weakness we see in ourselves and others, then we sink deeper into the world of form and move closer to the brink of annihilation along with our false identifications. If we insist upon judging the worthiness of others to receive our love, then there will not be enough love to save us in the days when breathing love is required for survival. We must all change our habits of perception with regard to each other, stop blaming each other for being less than perfect, and open ourselves to direct communion with the Essence of all those with whom we come in contact. Only in this way will this earth become a habitable place for the Shining One to dwell.

All relationships are primary vehicles through which Spirit does Its work. Each of us is an agent of Creation, and each relationship we form with any other agent of Creation constitutes the channel through which Creation proceeds. When these channels become clogged through our judgements of each other, our lack of forgiveness or compassion, the natural creativity we have been given with which to play our part gets diverted toward building barriers of separation. The ongoing process of Creation momentarily breaks down, and our entire planetary culture suffers consequences inimical to life.

Ultimately it is on the level of our relationships that the real work of healing the earth is to be done. It is in the relationships between lovers, husbands and wives, parents and children, employers and employees, teachers and students, that we all awaken to our common destiny. It is face to face with those we love, and those we hate, working out those issues that inevitably come between us, that the work of Creation proceeds, that Spirit incarnates more fully in this human form.

We can help each other tremendously in this awakening process by appreciating and encouraging the emergence of godbeing in each other. Through our words, our sharing of perceptions, our willingness to be mirrors for each other, and our unconditional acceptance of each other's growing pains, we heal the wounds of separation between us and create a space for our inviolable connection in Spirit to become the dominant reality between us.

After all, what are we but shattered fragments of the same Mirror, reflecting the same Light, endlessly recycled, bouncing back and forth between ourselves the wholeness we once knew before We split off into fragments. What now seems to be a problem for one of us is yesterday's crisis for someone else, and tomorrow's rite of passage for someone else again. Within each one of us, the entire cosmic drama of wholeness, fragmentation, and return to wholeness is re-enacted anew, as though each of us were the Only One. Yet, because there is more than one of us re-enacting this drama, we have the opportunity to learn from the struggles of each other what we can't always clearly extract from our own, and find clues in better lit corners of the maze than we have direct access to through our own experience.

Let us not be afraid, then, as we feel our vulnerability. Let us feel instead the company of our teachers around us, our mirrors, also vulnerable, yet willing to endure their vulnerability for the sake of the learning to be found in their mistakes. In this growing recognition among newly emergent godbeings, freshly awakened to a glimpse of common purpose, will come the planetary healing we all long for in our hearts.

As more and more of us around the globe experience planetary healing through the healing of our relationships, we shall gradually begin to realize that we are adjacent and interconnected cells within One Planetary Being. There is far more that we hold in common through our interconnectedness than any number of distinctions our mind can create to perpetuate the illusion of separation. As this realization eventually becomes the prevailing social paradigm, the divine plan underlying this Creation will become the blueprint from which we build a more sustainable, and satisfying future.

20

HEEDING THE CALL TO SERVICE

The planetary culture, so long defined in terms of individual differences and categories of separation, is now undergoing re-definition according to that which connects us to the greater whole. As such reconnections are made around the planet, whole societies will begin moving toward the creation of new social structures based on threads of unification, rather than separative distinctions. In this way, the relationship of the individual to society will change to permit more spontaneous, more frequent, and more powerful transmissions of divine grace and guidance to increasing numbers of people.

As we make this qualitative shift, it will necessarily be a time of introspection and self-evaluation. The age-old question, "Who am I?" will take on a new level of cosmic ramification as answers begin coming from a trans-human perspective in order to meet the challenge of planetary crises.

Nothing will satisfy in this new, intensified quest for self-understanding, except what takes into account our most divine attributes *and* points toward salvation for us all.

No one who settles for less of an answer than what promises to connect the individual to the planetary whole, will escape the battle of competitive elements that clears a space for such connections to proliferate. No one who lives in willful ignorance of her connection to the planetary process will survive. This is, in fact, the process of apocalypse by which the planetary slate will be cleared of fearful resistance to the movement of Spirit through form.

Thus, in this time of impelling human destiny, although the questions we ask are critical, the answers we are willing to accept are even more so.

Those who ask these deeper questions and respond from comparable depth will find themselves establishing inner connections to other dimensions we are connected to, but where we have not yet found our roots. Dreams will intensify. Visitations by felt "presences" from other realities, other solar systems, and archetypal corners of human consciousness will become more commonplace.

Communication with other species will alter forever our anthropomorphic perspective. Frequent encounters with angels, devas, and nature spirits will lead to miraculous activation of higher biological potentials. Signs, omens, and unmistakable revelations of the more cosmic understrata of surface activity will abound for those capable of reading them.

There is in fact, no point of receptivity in any of the many realms where consciousness can be said to exist that will not be touched in some way by the movement toward unification and connectedness being precipitated at this time. Thus, even as the accumulated tension of widespread fear, paranoid anger, and the rampant abuse of power threatens to consume us, a divine effort toward counterbalancing proceeds with special vigor, and spreads its own web of protection to delicate and detailed capillary intricacy. To participate in this counterbalancing, we need only proceed with clear intention to make the essential connection between the personal and the planetary sphere.

The rest will come of its own accord.

Individual paths of work, social activity, and spiritual development, are now being more sharply attuned to an emerging planetary ethic, and the pressure is upon us all to begin to seek personal fulfillment through service to the greater whole. The more one is focused on one's own self-gratification, the greater the sense of restriction, and of being compelled toward a reality outside one's control. The more attuned to cooperative ventures, on the other hand, the more defined one's specific role within the greater whole becomes, and the more powerful the opening through restriction and chaos into a heightened sense of co-creativity and purpose.

It is time to put ourselves on the line, standing firm for what we believe in, demonstrating to others those values we are willing to fight for, or in some sense, sacrifice our lives to uphold. The time for empty words, or even good intentions has past. It is time now to act upon what we have long felt within our hearts, sharing ourselves through some definite service to our brothers and sisters, and to the planet itself.

Let our thoughts and words be clear. Let our intentions be pure. Let our actions be to the point and effective in attaining their goal. If each of us takes our inner voice to heart, and actually pays it heed, more will be accomplished toward ushering a new age of peace, balance, and equitable abundance into our lives than all the words we have spoken, and all the good intentions we have had since we became conscious enough to want this new age for our garden planet. Let us forget the inertia that has heretofore held us back. Let us not let our jargon and our auras of spirituality get in our way. Let us let go of the conveniences we have allowed to become our excuse. Let us actually do what we have long known deep down in our souls we must do.

It is possible we have felt powerless in the face of impossible odds; felt dwarfed by the concentration of earthly power in remote corporations, government agencies, and public institutions; felt overwhelmed by the sheer inertia of human history; felt intimidated by the sophistication and accelerating complexity of our technology; felt insignificant against the vast hordes of seemingly uncaring, self-centered, short-sighted servants to the Beast; or simply felt unclear about where to begin to make an impact. These are all feelings that carry great weight and bear deep scrutiny, but perhaps some other time.

Let us put aside the valid, but largely unanswerable questions that arise as we ponder these feelings, and focus on something closer to home and more manageable in the here and now of our daily lives.

What is it right now that most deeply touches our lives, that drives us toward our most profound changes, captures our passion, permeates our dreams and our stolen moments? What calls us from within, as well as from the world outside ourselves, and begs to be given the time and energy we now spend attending to our survival needs? What is the seed impulse that gave rise to our lives in the first place, made it worth the mixed blessing of human birth, tore us from the freedom of our spaceless, timeless existence in the spirit world to clothe ourselves in matter and age? What is the chord that rings out through the heavens as the angels chant our holy name in homage to our mission here on earth? Who are we, and what have we come here to do? We may have forgotten, but we will remember. We may have gotten lost, but we will find our way again. We must, for in this remembering lies our power - the only power we have - to effect change, to make a significant difference, to play our vital part in the healing of the earth.

Nor is this remembering very far away. In reality, it is at your fingertips. What feels important to you now? At the heart of this sensing lies a pure impulse. To take one small, but significant step toward the healing of the earth, take this pure impulse, and make it *the* priority in your life. Go ahead. Don't be shy.

You are being called toward a higher destiny. Who are you to refuse? Not ready yet? Why not trust that Spirit has worked overtime your entire life to prepare you for this very moment, this mission that lies before you? You cannot possibly fail.

Who is knocking on your door? What are they asking you for? At the heart of their request lies a pure, legitimate need. To take one small, but significant step toward serving this Creation, take this request and make it your command. Why not? Too busy doing other things? Why not assume that time is precious, and that fulfilling your purpose in this life hangs upon your successful completion of this small act of giving? How can you refuse? No need to make the healing of the planet, or serving others more complicated than it is.

Waves upon waves of loving, healing, enlightening energy ripple out into the world from the center of each small heartfelt act of giving. Don't wonder who, what, where, when, how to serve. Just remain open. Whoever it is that can benefit by what you have to give will find their way to your doorstep. They will ask you for what they want, when they need it. You will know how to serve them, because you have prepared all your life to be who you already are.

In the cosmic balance sheet, Spirit's gift to you is Being. Being yourself is all Spirit will ever ask in return. It is all you can ever give and all anyone can ever receive from you. All else is simply manipulation or showmanship. Don't worry that your actions will not touch enough people in enough time to matter. You are not alone, and the more you give what is there to be given, the more connected you are to the dispensation of divine grace that is everywhere now touching the planet with its blessing.

Don't worry that technology will turn against us in the end. Before and after technology has done all it can do for better or worse, it is only the technology of human caring that will determine the success or failure of this experiment we conduct on earth.

Don't worry that the inertia of history belies our best effort. It is our best effort that will fill the next page of the living history that we pass down to our children and our children's children, even if distortion does fill the written book yet for awhile.

Don't feel insignificant in the face of concentrated power. The act of Creation was, and is an act of Love. All power that derives from some other source will fade in the brilliance of the Shining One's Presence.

Don't worry that the odds of turning the tide of human misery, suffering, and long-standing drift toward oblivion seem impossible. How impossible is it that we are here now, sharing these words, when just a few short blinks of the Cosmic Eye ago, there was nothing - no you, no me, no computer on which to type this message, no language, no civilization, no planet, no solar system - nothing.

It is not an idle exercise that carries us this far.

It will not be an idle exercise that determines our fate.

We have been created for this moment. Let us take this moment and give it back to Spirit by being who we have been created to be.

In and of ourselves we can perhaps accomplish nothing, but there is no limitation the Shining One within us has not already surpassed. In the end, we will only marvel at the wonders Spirit accomplishes through the vehicle we provide.

It is time to humble ourselves before the flow of Spirit, taking less credit for what gets done through us, while opening ourselves to do more. With or without our help, the old social order will be transformed to accommodate the Shining One seeking to be born. Yet, as we open ourselves in consciousness to prepare the way for this new age of co-creative service, a place within this world is prepared for us. Whatever obstacles within the old world crumbling would otherwise stand in our way will be removed as an act of grace.

21

THE CHANGING NATURE
OF THE POWER GAME

Each of us has a direct inviolable connection to the Source of our Being, and need look no further for our sustenance and well-being. It is through this connection that we experience the only power we have to effect meaningful change. Although it is easy to become awed at the concentration of power we see in government, multi-national corporations, banks, and other public institutions, the truth is that each of us has access to every bit as much power through our own essential divinity.

History, it can be argued, is the story of power and privilege as it has been claimed by the few, and used to dominate or control the many. But history is not often seen to be the cosmic process that it is, with the misleading result that the superficial flow of events is often given too much emphasis.

What has actually been happening, on the level on which divine plan unfolds is that the Source of All Power has been gradually stepping up the voltage of power available, thereby rendering it manageable only in the hands of those who can use it consciously. Where power has been used for the sole purpose of propping up small identity, to manipulate or infringe upon the rights of others, or to upset ecological balance, it has had obvious long-term repercussions inimical to life. As increasingly disastrous mistakes are made, consciousness slowly rises.

It is likely, in the days ahead, that many of those who abuse power in these ways will find that power suddenly cut off. Such a dramatic and powerful reversal of fortune will occur, not because power is taken away, or usurped by someone else, but because more and more people around the planet are reawakening to the truth of their own connection to the Source of Power, and revitalizing that connection through obedience to the inner voice of self-actualization.

THE BIRTH OF THE SHINING ONE

As the emergence of godbeing everywhere generates an atmosphere in which high level creativity and the skillful use of power for purposes in accord with the design of Spirit become the norm, the abuse of power that has previously plagued our history will simply not be possible.

Those who are centered within their own power can not be dominated by others. Those for whom the experience of interconnection with the entire web of life is a sacred fact of daily life will simply not tolerate senseless desecration of the environment. Those who have learned to channel the abundance of this universe cannot be manipulated by fear of scarcity or lack.

Without cooperation; without a general willingness to support the illusion of powerlessness, those that attempt to consolidate and abuse power will be without the means to do so. The power games that have distracted so many from the actualization of their true purpose will no longer be attractive. The consolidation of power for purely selfish purposes will be a meaningless pursuit that only serves to isolate would-be tyrants and bullies from the rest of the world.

At a time when the strengthening of individuality was the focal point for human evolution, a wide latitude for the abuse of personal power was allowed so that many valuable lessons could be learned. Now, however, as the divine plan requires a higher level of cooperation between individuals, groups, nations, and races, individuality is important, not so much for the sake of individuals, as for the sake of the whole to which the individual belongs. The effective exercise of power will increasingly depend upon cooperation, goodwill, and attunement to a vision that engages the integrated peak creativity of large numbers of people.

Whole societies of godbeings will operate at a level of productivity simply not possible where the myth of powerlessness prevails.

Grand and glorious transformations will probably not take place overnight, but as the vibrational intensity of planetary transformation steadily builds, self-empowerment will become the everday experience of "ordinary" people, and the ways in which power is experienced will change. The focus of attention will gradually shift from who has power in the moment to where power ultimately comes from. Power will no longer be seen as something to be bought, fought for, or exercised over other people, but as the birthright of us all. As these shifts in attitude are made around the planet, those who previously vied amongst themselves for power will begin to find common interest in clearer perception of their true relationship to the Source of Power they each independently sought to monopolize.

The power that is available to every one of us is a natural expression of our godbeing. There is literally nothing that one who is centered in godbeing cannot do because godbeing moves in accordance with divine intention, and has the omnipotence of Spirit behind it. At the Core of our being, we are the Source of All Power, although we have all been trained to vigorously deny this truth.

We have shied away from our omnipotence in the past because we were intimidated by the responsibility we believed omnipotence required. We falsely confused this responsibility with control of circumstances, and naturally experienced our confusion as the limitation of our power.

There was (and is) no way we could control every circumstance of our own lives, never mind those affecting planetary process. There was (and is) no way we could solve every problem the world would ever be challenged by.

Wherever we encountered a situation beyond our control, or met a problem we did not know how to deal with, we lapsed into powerlessness. We projected our power onto God, or the government, or our partner, or the enemy.

Except for a few megalomaniacs who have tortured history with their folly, it rarely enters human consciousness to assume the level of responsibility we have associated with omnipotence. This world was not designed to be saved by one individual, or even a group of individuals controlling planetary circumstances. It was created to actualize the godbeing within us all, as we, in turn, worked together to actualize the godbeing of the earth.

The responsibility demanded by godbeing, however, is not the responsibility we have associated with omnipotence.

It has nothing to do with control of cirumstances. It is rather an expression of our our willingness to be who we are, in all the manifest power of our innocence, to dare to look at life with fresh eyes, to think for ourselves, to appreciate the beauty that dwells inside this magnificent creation, and to live the truth that we find in our hearts.

Our responsibility to the planet is ultimately no different that the responsibility we feel toward our own highest sense of integrity, for when we move from that place of integrity, we move in accordance with the divine plan for this earth.

Ultimately, the responsibility of godbeing is the very antithesis of control, for in order to honor our own integrity, we must relinquish our need to control others, or the world around us. The exercise of godbeing requires a higher level of trust, where energy previously rooted in fear and insecurity and bound by patterns of control is freed to move in sync with the heartbeat of the mystery unfolding. We need not know what comes next, or try to control the outcome of our actions, we need only give our consent to Spirit moving through us in the present moment, and trust that our actions have their place within divine intention. We must assume the existence of a divine plan for this earth, and deeply feel our part within this plan.

We must act from a place of truthfulness and attunement, not from a place of fear.

If we are moved to respond to some environmental crisis, we must do so, not because we fear toxic contamination, but because we see clearly in our hearts that the divine plan for this planet requires clean air, water, and soil. If we are inspired to extend our compassion to other human beings, it must not be because we feel superior or at advantage, but because we see the godbeing in them trying to emerge and feel honored to participate in that miracle. If we should be called to the political arena, we must not seek glory, but rather stand firm in the awareness of the divine intention we wish to anchor. If our calling is to fill some humbler station, it must not be because we believe we have no other options, but because our sense of purpose calls us there.

The power of godbeing is not dependent upon appearances or the judgement of the world, but on the strength of inner connection. This connection, unique to each of us, cannot be seen or judged by external standards, but it will be felt wherever it becomes the basis for a life. Where godbeing is expressed, the omnipotence of Spirit moves, and the outer forms through which it passes automatically expand to accomodate the higher voltage.

Unlike the power we have seen abused by small identity, the power of godbeing requires a commensurate exercise of consciousness. We cannot claim this power without first realizing our interconnectedness with each other and our integrated place within the whole web of life. We must feel the magnitude of the mystery that permeates this planetary sphere, and realize with humility the precious nature of the task we have been given. We must surrender whatever attachments we have to small identity, so that Spirit might move through us unencumbered by powerlessness or fear. We must make room for the movement of omnipotence through our lives, without succumbing to illusions of grandiosity. We must learn to recognize the emerging godbeing in each other, and draw that godbeing forth through our love and mirroring.

The power of godbeing is a power that must be shared, for it is only through cooperation that the responsibility of omnipotence can be handled. This is not a responsibility we must figure out with our rational minds, or scheme to fulfill through the exercise of control. It is a responsibility that must be surrendered to in awe of mystery, and carried out through a leap of faith in the power that is our birthright. It is one we can only meet as we maintain the focus of our own integrity in the holy company of others doing likewise. Then, as each of us claims our godbeing, and orients our lives around its creative momentum, what we do to fulfill ourselves will automatically contribute to the good of the whole. The whole, in turn, illuminated by the creative renaissance of millions of awakening individuals, will nurture and support the awakening and fulfillment of millions more and set this entire planetary sphere aglow.

22

BUILDING A VIBRATIONAL WEB OF PLANETARY PROTECTION

As ever increasing numbers of us commit ourselves to the healing of planetary life support systems, a vibrational atmosphere is established where it becomes increasingly difficult to make decisions that adversely affect this process. As we each play the part we are inspired to play, the intensity of our collective focus will generate a widespread network of protection in which we can more easily do our work.

Those now making decisions on the basis of short-term economic gain, or the consolidation of political power, at the expense of ecological balance, or human freedom, will find it increasingly difficult to justify their actions.

There will be little support for such unconscious and dangerous policies as this vibrational atmosphere of communion with the divine plan encompasses the earth in its protective web. Each time we withdraw support from those who endanger life, deny human freedom or stifle creativity, and turn our energy to the construction of positive alternatives, we strengthen this web of protection, and help generate an atmosphere where the work of those who would destroy the earth in their ignorance and greed becomes increasingly untenable.

As builders of the vibrational web, we can tap into an unlimited reservoir of strength and creativity that will enable us to do our jobs with dexterity, resourcefulness, and poignancy. This reservoir is always available to us, as it is ultimately the Source of our Being and our Life. In the days to come, however, those of us consciously working to support Life will find a wider avenue of access to this reservoir, while those who lust after money and power, while flirting with death, will find their access narrowed.

THE BIRTH OF THE SHINING ONE

Life, after all, wishes to continue to unfold in Its expression of divine beauty, to glorify the unfathomable mystery of the Creator delighting in Creation. And so, as those who play the poker game of death step up the intensity of their efforts, Life becomes the Cosmic Monkeywrencher, rigging decks, marking cards, cheating and beating the despoilers at their own game, while lending an unseen hand to those who have taken it upon themselves to build the protective web. We, who have consciously placed ourselves on the side of life, should be gratified to know we have such an ingenious and wonderfully mischievous teammate as the Cosmic Monkeywrencher to help us. With the Monkeywrencher battling those gearing up for battle, we need not focus our energies in ways that contribute to the atmosphere of battle, but can instead concentrate on the building of forms more appropriate to the nurturance of life.

Ultimately, it is through the power of nurturance that the vibrational web that protects the earth will be built.

As we give our bodies, minds, and hearts what they need to work in harmony as a vehicle for the expression of divine purpose, we are able to project the energy of loving nurturance outward into the world we inhabit. As we honor the godbeings in each other, and support each other in our work, we build a network of loving nurturance between us.

As we appreciate the Earth through our willingness to care for her living creatures, her precious soil, her waterways, the air She breathes, we pull this network of loving nurturance around us all, like a cloak against the storm.

Living, working, playing, loving, and building with this energy of nurturance, this cloak of protection against the storm becomes our covenant with Life.

As we maintain the web of life, so shall the Cosmic Monkeywrencher work to keep strong our protective cloak, and turn the storm away. As we intensify our efforts, sharpen our focus, hone our tools to optimum efficiency and effectiveness, so shall the Monkeywrencher mirror our efforts in taking care of His appointed task.

The Monkeywrencher, though, it should be pointed out in fairness, is a jealous and fastidious being, carefully insisting that none of His protected children interfere with or try to do His work. As soon as we divert our attention from the building of forms that nurture and foster life to battle those that prostitute themselves in death-dealing ways, we become the "enemy," and the Monkeywrencher moves with great stealth and cunning to sabotage our tangential efforts.

This is not to say that we should not confront those who have not yet attuned themselves to that level of appreciation for Life that will ensure the survival of this planet, for such confrontation is inevitable. As we withdraw our support from those organizations and institutions that facilitate death, and put our energies into the construction of positive alternatives, we cannot help but confront those who deal in death with the insanity of their ways. Our confrontation must be grounded, however, in the same loving nurturance that sustains our efforts toward planetary restoration, and include those we confront in the protective web we are building. Otherwise our confrontation only tears the fabric of that web. There is something much more important and vital going on than what appears to be happening on the level those who deal in death are operating from, and it is toward this underlying process of planetary revitalization that we must maintain our attention.

"Keep your focus," the Monkeywrencher constantly reminds us. "Keep your innocence, for the innocence which knows, without question, that the spark of Life cannot be extinguished, will never have to fear death. In the end, it will be death that battles death. Win or lose, Life will continue, and as you hold in consciousness, thought, word, and deed, the image of yourself as one who loves, honors, and nurtures Life, so, in one form or another, will you." Where we doubt and fear, the Cosmic Monkeywrencher will remind us through His sabotage that we stray from our true path. Where we one-pointedly pour our creative energies into building a new world based on love and nurturance, the Cosmic Monkeywrencher will draw His protective cloak around us, and shield us from the storm.

This is not to say that those of us conscious of the urgent need for change can afford to sit back and wait for our collective longing to fashion itself into a viable force. We must all do our part to ground our dreams in concrete action. For while it is true that this longing is the energy of salvation, it must be harnessed by a deliberate act of will to powerful images of peace, natural balance, and sustainability. These images must be given form and set in motion, so that the divine plan can anchor itself in earthly substance.

111

THE BIRTH OF THE SHINING ONE

We must all work hard toward creating tangible evidence for the viability of life-affirming alternatives, and fuel a positive momentum that our collective longing can attach itself to. In this way, our visions can come alive within the minds and hearts of even the most diehard skeptics. As we demonstrate the practicality of the divine plan in operation, options which support life will gain widespread acceptance and begin to replace those of short-sighted vision. The seed of divine intention will burst in glorious revelation through the bitter soil of battle to unite those who previously saw themselves fighting for antithetical ideals.

What now appears to separate and divide, will ultimately be understood as the force which brought us all together. What now appears to repress and contain the human spirit, will in the end be recognized to be the crucible in which our strength was born. What now appears to decimate and despoil, will one day be placed in historical perspective as providing the incentive humanity needed to embrace the road toward right stewardship.

It is time to begin sharing our visions for a peaceful, balanced, and sustainable future with those who daily imbibe the images of death. We must learn to include those who might not otherwise participate, in our most intimate acts of communion—without awkwardness, without embarrassment, without apology—as part of a natural flow between ourselves and the world of fear. New rituals of connection and inclusion will spontaneously suggest themselves, and communication deepen wherever that deep longing for life within us all can be spoken to. We must make the effort to reach out, to touch those afraid to touch, to teach those who lack awareness of the power of their godbeing, to balance the evidence of death with the evidence of our own life-light shining steadily. We must affirm the seed of pure intention within all that surrounds us. We must activate and direct the longing for life within the heart of humanity.

There is great joy looming just beneath the surface of despair. There is great power to release that joy within our work on behalf of this planet. There is great need to recognize and affirm that power in ourselves and in everyone we meet. Let us not shrink before what appears to be the skulk of death in our neighborhood. Let us remember that the Cosmic Monkeywrencher works diligently on our behalf.

Let us celebrate the life-and-death realities that push us toward the brink of self-annihilation, because in the end, they will only serve to draw forth our creative capacities toward self-salvation and salvation of the planet.

23

REACHING TOWARD DIVINITY IN HUMAN FORM

We are about to make a rapid turn upon the evolutionary spiral, the magnitude of which cannot be imagined in the mere measure of each small change we can perceive with our senses. We are, in a sense, building a platform raised high above the ground, a carefully planned, well constructed foundation upon which communion with the gods becomes not only possible, but inevitable. This platform, raised to meet the gods midway between the human and the divine, will be built according to ancient instructions encoded etherically at the dawn of human consciousness. In a sense, the platform to be built has already been built, has always existed on the etheric plane, waiting for the appropriate time to come into tangible manifestation. Now that time has come.

As we all come together to participate in the construction of this primordial reality, deep memories will be stirred. We will once again remember what was set in motion so very long ago. Excitement will mount as a long lost ancient truth is rediscovered. There will also be a few surprises, as human free will has since altered the ancient plan, and nature does not always reveal its deepest secrets from the start.

As the building begins, many of the plans that have been so carefully constructed and maintained by the human mind will dissolve in irrelevance. To this point, we have considered ourselves to be conscious in our deliberate movement toward particular horizons. What will become clear, however, as the building of the platform begins, is that we have, in fact, been moving somnambulistically through a dream toward horizons we would balk at were we conscious enough to protest.

Because the human nervous system has not yet evolved to the point where the reality it is designed to channel can be actively experienced, we have been lead toward that reality with the temporary help of certain illusions skillfully imbedded at the core of our perceptual mechanisms. In this way, we have been lead to do certain things, both collectively and as individuals, that we would not otherwise do. Our conscious intentions were ones that made sense to us, but were in reality beside the point. Now, however, as the time for the building of the platform is upon us, it is also time for these temporary illusions we have relied on for so long to be lifted. It is time for the real purpose of our existence to be revealed directly and unfiltered.

Such revelation will take place in the building of the tower that is to hold the platform itself. At each stage of the scaffolding process, many individuals will be lost to the unfathomability of what is revealed to them. This unfathomability will breed terror where innocence has not been reclaimed. Where Creation is viewed through eyes blinded by mindsets, destruction will be perceived. Those locked into frozen images, will see only the enemy advancing. They will perhaps fight with great courage, and be hailed as heroes by those who share their blindness, but in the end, they will fall from the tower into the fires of creativity below, where old form is destroyed and energy released for the work of building above.

Those that are left, those that are pure enough, true enough to their own passion, willing to look at what is happening with the eyes of innocence, strong enough to withstand the mounting vibrational pressures all around them, will then climb higher to erect the next stage of the scaffolding. By the time the platform itself is raised, only the purest, the truest, the most innocent, the strongest will remain to do the intricate esoteric work that remains. This work will then provide the foundation in consciousness for the renaissance of Spirit that is to follow.

Progressively higher levels of scaffolding will require increasingly higher levels of coordination and cooperation among individuals working to help one another and to bring about a common goal. At the earlier stages, the cooperation may well be a matter of convenience or expediency, but as we move together more deeply into the mystery, we will cooperate more consciously in attunement with the divine plan underlying this Creation.

Though the whole plan will not be revealed until the very last stages of construction, there will be increasing joy and celebration as each piece of the puzzle falls into place. There will be a strong sense of ritual about the work. Outwardly mundane tasks will take on vibrant symbolic significance as steps within a silent dance of re-enactment and communion. Those who participate most deeply in this work will move about within a constant state of deja vu. All who participate will be moved to abandon small identity for more complete immersion in timeless patterns.

It is time to understand and heed the calling in our hearts, and take our place in the construction crew. The platform, already shimmering in etheric outline, calls out for manifestation on this earthly plane, calls out for each and every soul to reclaim the power of innocence, and join in the work at hand. As we lighten our burden of identification with circumstances, and help each other to do likewise, the scaffolding rises of its own accord. As we tighten our commitment to our true purpose here on earth, the tower becomes strong and vibrant. As we reach with every fiber of our being toward a new order of godbeing within human form, we become reconnected to an ancient truth born again through us. As we honor our own integrity with empowered action, we restore the garden paradise this planet was created to be.

Even for those with no awareness of the spiritual dimension of their reality, the emergence of the Shining One is being felt. It is no accident the pressure of life and death technology is now forcing us all to reassess the very meaning of life, and move toward closer identification with the quickening pulse of the human heartbeat. Because we are faced with the possibility of massive annihilation of our life support systems, and extinction as a species, life within the moment becomes precious, and true communion among neighbors the unspoken focus of all interaction. In the scramble for reassurance, feelings are more easily shared, and issues of more than superficial importance replace mere chit-chat as the staple of discussion. Deeper bonds of friendship and co-creativity move us all toward more rapid transformation. Because of shared longing for a planet that is healed, we are all attuning ourselves to the real possibilities for our survival. We are all more willing to trade the small measure of security circumstances have been able to provide for more intimate participation in the planetary process. As collective danger mounts, priorities are rearranged.

Little of this planetary process is ever reflected through the eyes of our media. Even the most astute observations of those caught up in identification with circumstance and form often miss the point. Such observations belong to a surface world, and cannot begin to approach the level upon which the real magnitude and nature of planetary process reveals itself.

Those of us who would touch the heart of this process must dive deeper, and free ourselves of the false security provided by what seems obvious. Being able to explain what is happening in rational terms is less important now than our willingness to hear what makes no logical sense but intuitively feels right.

Now is not the time to indulge the cultural trance of business as usual, or lock ourselves into patterns of limitation. It is only those who keep themselves free to dance to the music of the inner ear, follow the distant calling of the mystery, and fly upon the wings of spontaneity who will survive this planetary rite of passage. Let us all move into position to do the greatest good we are capable of doing, and let us all move with joy in our hearts. Let us all dance to the song of remembering.

Let us all reach beyond the apocalypse that threatens this fragile world of form, and create a new world where the godbeing within each of us is cherished and drawn forth.

Let us give conscious birth to the Shining One arising in our midst.

EPILOGUE: PLANTING THE STARGARDEN

As you awaken, rubbing the sleep of countless centuries from your eyes, the world you have created begins to glow with a definite light of its own. The very stones you walk upon speak with a wisdom no earthly master ever possessed.

The trees of antiquity that escaped the cutting blade your children wielded in their ignorance, now arch from earth to heaven, visible shafts of luminescent connection. The flowers you touch in passing sing a symphony of welcome.

Eagles paint iridescent rainbows with their wings.

All around you, godbeings join hands in celebration of Your coming. Long since having left the weapons of separation to rust in the fields of human folly, these godbeings now generate an aura of peace and dancing innocence. Wise beyond their appearance of guileless wonder, they have created communities of trust and caring in which You will permanently dwell. Listen, they call to You now with open hearts and minds.

You have come to reward them for an experiment successfully completed. You have come to bless them with entry to the greater mysteries available to consciousness within physical form. You have come to release them from the last threads of their bondage. They look to You now with shining eyes, as they see only the Identity they have so deeply longed for. Many weep for joy. Many laugh with abandon. All are grateful for Your abiding Presence within them and around them.

You are also released through Your Identity in Them, for They are Your children grown beyond the fear of death that plagued them long ago. They have survived a dangerous passage, and emerged with innocence intact. They have rediscovered their power and learned to use it wisely. They have proven themselves worthy of a larger mission. You are proud of Them, and enfold them in Your Smile.

Holding hands around the circle now, You sing the ancient song of release and liberation. The last veils of separation dissolve in a shimmering bow to magical intention. Cells within a Planetary Body coalesce in Ecstasy. One small bounce, and wings of uncommon delight unfurl in magnificence and wonder. Homeward bound, You wink lovingly at your garden planet cradle, untold galaxies kissing in the twinkle of Your eye. All are born again in You, as human seeds of Godbeing sprout joyously in Your image upon countless worlds throughout the stargarden of endless space.

Joe Landwehr, an astrologer living in New Mexico, is a bright new star in Uni★Sun's constellation of writers. We hope to see his work again soon.

In the meantime, we at Uni★Sun will do our best to publish books and offer products that make a real contribution to the global spiritual awakening that has already begun on this planet. For a free copy of our catalogue, please write to:

Uni★Sun
P.O. Box 25421
Kansas City, Missouri
64119
U.S.A.